Nancy Mahoney

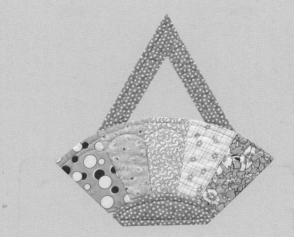

APPLIQUÉ QUILT REVIVAL

Updated Patterns from the '30s

Martingale®
& COMPANY

Appliqué Quilt Revival:
Updated Patterns from the '30s
© 2008 by Nancy Mahoney

That Patchwork Place® is an imprint
of Martingale & Company®.

Martingale & Company
20205 144th Ave. NE
Woodinville, WA 98072-8478 USA
www.martingale-pub.com

Credits

President & CEO ◆ Tom Wierzbicki
Publisher ◆ Jane Hamada
Editorial Director ◆ Mary V. Green
Managing Editor ◆ Tina Cook
Technical Editor ◆ Ellen Pahl
Copy Editor ◆ Melissa Bryan
Design Director ◆ Stan Green
Production Manager ◆ Regina Girard
Illustrator ◆ Robin Strobel
Cover Designer ◆ Stan Green
Text Designer ◆ Regina Girard
Photographer ◆ Brent Kane

Printed in China
13 12 11 10 09 08   8 7 6 5 4 3 2 1

Library of Congress Cataloging-in-Publication Data
is available upon request.

ISBN: 978-1-56477-822-2

Mission Statement

*Dedicated to providing quality products
and service to inspire creativity.*

CONTENTS

INTRODUCTION

Quilt patterns appeared in dozens of newspapers in the 1930s. Many newspapers offered the patterns for sale through their "Household Arts Department," but forwarded their orders to a pattern source in a major city such as San Francisco or New York. One of these sources was Needlecraft Services, which began offering single full-size quilt patterns through the mail in 1932. The New York address of Needlecraft Services was located in the same neighborhood as the Old Chelsea Station (OCS) post office. In that era before zip codes, Old Chelsea Station, New York City, was enough to direct the pattern request to the right place. As a result, the "Old Chelsea Station" name was given to a series of patterns. Thrifty quilters collected these patterns, but the patterns were also traded, shared, tried, and loved over and over again.

Independent pattern studios published syndicated columns under the names Alice Brooks, Laura Wheeler, Aunt Martha, and Carol Curtis. Although these authors were fictional, their names gave a personal touch to the quilt designs. Favorite traditional patterns were rediscovered and modified in the 1920s and 1930s, while some patterns, such as Double Wedding Ring, appeared for the first time. Realistic-looking appliqué patterns, rather than abstract flowers and images, became popular during this period; a rose looked like a rose.

Children's quilts with a juvenile theme also became popular, reaching a peak during the 1930s. Sunbonnet Sue, a favorite children's design, first appeared as an appliqué pattern during this period, although this beloved design had been used as an outline embroidery design in the nineteenth century.

The most common colors seen in 1930s quilts are pale-yellowish " '30s green" (also called Nile green), pink, orchid, buttery yellow, and light blue. Red, bluish green, peach, soft brown or tan, and black also appear in quilts from this period. These modern pastels and cheerful color schemes became synonymous with floral appliqué. Most of the quilts were scrap-bag style; all kinds of prints and colors were combined and then pulled together with white or other solids.

At the beginning of the twentieth century, creativity flourished as quilters embraced new quilt designs and technologies. As quilters of the twenty-first century, we have an even greater variety of new ideas and techniques at our fingertips.

Here, I've selected 12 appliqué patterns from my collection of vintage '30s quilt patterns to create 14 charming appliqué projects. As in my book *Quilt Revival* (Martingale & Company, 2006), the projects in these pages are scrappy in style, constructed with '30s reproduction fabrics, but they make use of updated appliqué and piecing techniques. These wonderful, homey quilts offer something for everyone: delightful bunnies, cheery flowerpots, darling kittens, beautiful butterflies, stunning wreaths, and frolicking cowboys.

So grab your scrap bag—you're sure to have fun making these cheerful quilts.

~ Nancy

On the pages that follow, you will find valuable information for the successful completion of your quilt. All the special techniques needed to complete your quilt are covered in this section.

▦ ROTARY CUTTING

The projects in this book are all designed for rotary cutting and are easily pieced by machine. Use your cutter to cut block backgrounds and borders as well as the patchwork strips and pieces in your project. All rotary-cutting measurements include ¼"-wide seam allowances. Basic rotary-cutting tools include a rotary cutter, an 18" x 24" cutting mat, a 6" x 24" acrylic ruler, and a 12½" square ruler for trimming appliqué blocks. You'll be able to make all the projects with these rulers, although I also find a 6" Bias Square® very useful for making cleanup cuts and crosscutting squares from strips.

▦ CUTTING STRAIGHT STRIPS

Cutting strips at an exact right angle to the folded edge of your fabric is essential for accuracy. Rotary cutting squares, rectangles, and other shapes begins with cutting accurate strips. Note that the rotary-cutting instructions are written for right-handers; reverse the instructions if you are left-handed.

Begin by pressing the fabric and then folding it in half with the selvages together. Place the fabric on your cutting mat with the folded edge nearest to your body. Align the Bias Square ruler with the fold of the fabric and place a 6" x 24" ruler to the left so that the raw edges of the fabric are covered.

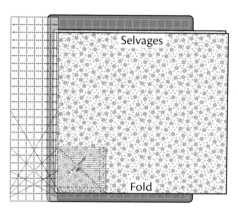

Remove the Bias Square and make a rotary cut along the right side of the long ruler. Remove the long ruler and gently remove the waste strip. This is known as a cleanup cut.

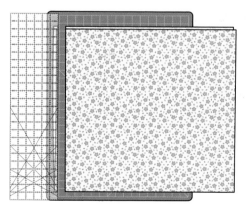

To cut strips, align the desired strip-width measurement on the ruler with the cut edge of the fabric and carefully cut the strip. After cutting three or four strips, realign the Bias Square along the fold and make a new cleanup cut.

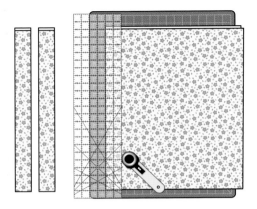

CUTTING SQUARES AND RECTANGLES

To cut squares and rectangles, cut strips in the desired widths. Cut the selvage ends off the strip in the same way that you made the cleanup cut. Align the required measurements on the ruler with the left edge of the strip and cut a square or rectangle. Continue cutting until you have the required number of pieces.

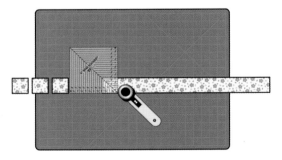

MACHINE PIECING

The most important aspect of machine piecing is to maintain an accurate ¼" seam allowance. This enables all the seams to match and the blocks to fit together properly. Line up the cut edges of your fabric pieces precisely and stitch. Backstitching is not necessary, since the seams will cross each other.

When sewing several identical fabric pieces together, I like to chain piece the patches to save time. To chain piece, sew the first pair of patches together. At the end of the seam line, stop sewing but do not cut the thread. Feed the next pair of patches under the pressure foot and continue sewing in the same manner until all the patches are sewn. Remove the chain of patches from the machine and clip the threads between the pairs of sewn patches as you press them.

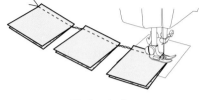

Chain piecing

PRESSING

Pressing is one of the keys to precise piecing. It is important to carefully press your work after stitching each seam. Pressing is planned so that the seam allowances will oppose one another when you sew the blocks and rows together. Pressing directions are provided with each project.

Set your iron on the cotton setting and use a padded pressing surface to prevent the seam allowance from creating a ridge on the right side of the unit. Use a pressing cloth when ironing raised areas with multiple seams (which protects your fabrics from becoming glazed and shiny under the iron). To avoid possible distortion, allow the pieces to cool before moving them from the pressing surface.

Long Seams

When pressing long seams, first press the seam flat from the wrong side to smooth out any puckers. Be sure to use an up-and-down motion, rather than the back-and-forth, gliding motion typical of ironing, to avoid stretching the fabric. Open the sewn unit and, from the right side, press in the direction indicated in the project diagram. Use the tip of the iron to gently push the fabric over the seam.

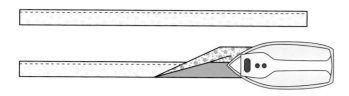

SQUARING UP BLOCKS

After you've stitched the appliqués onto the block backgrounds, you need to square up the block, keeping the design centered. To square up an appliqué block, line up the vertical and horizontal centerlines of the block with the centerlines of the desired size square on the square ruler. For example, the centerline of a 9" square is the 4½" line. Cut the first two sides of the square. Turn the block around and cut the other two sides.

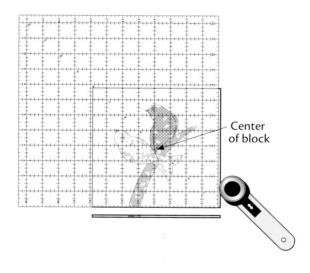

Center of block

APPLIQUÉ TECHNIQUES

There are many ways to appliqué—both by hand and by machine. Each method uses different techniques. Before starting an appliqué project, you can choose which method is best for that particular project. If you are making a special heirloom quilt, you may want to use a hand-appliqué method. If, however, you are making a quilt that will receive hard wear, machine appliqué is often the best and most efficient choice. Or you may find you'll want to use a combination of methods or techniques.

Cutting Background Fabric

All appliqué patterns in this book are printed at full size. Because appliqué blocks tend to distort slightly and fray during stitching, you will cut the block backgrounds 1" larger than the finished size and trim them to the correct size after completing the appliqué. For instance, for a 9" finished block, the background fabric would normally be cut 9½" x 9½" to allow for ¼" seam allowance on all sides. For appliqué, the block background is cut 10" x 10" and then trimmed to 9½" x 9½". Use a rotary cutter, mat, and acrylic ruler to accurately cut the blocks.

Once you've cut your block backgrounds, mark the center of each piece. You can fold the piece in half vertically and horizontally and lightly press to create centerlines. However, I prefer to use a pencil and ruler to lightly mark the center on the *wrong side* of the background piece. I use the center mark to position my appliqué pieces. Then, when the appliqué is complete, I can use the same marks to square up the block.

Wrong side of fabric

+

Mark the center.

Making Appliqué Templates

Since you'll be making more than one of each appliqué piece, you'll find it handy to make a plastic template for each pattern piece. Templates made from clear or frosted plastic are durable and accurate, and because you can see through the plastic, you can easily trace the shapes from the patterns. You can trace the pieces of each appliqué design directly from the pattern to create the templates you'll need. Seam allowances are not included on templates for appliqué pieces. Prepare your templates accurately to ensure the best results.

To make the templates, place template plastic over each pattern piece and trace with a fine-line permanent marker, making sure to trace the lines exactly. Do not add a seam allowance. Use utility scissors to cut out the templates, cutting exactly on the drawn lines. Write the block name and pattern number on the template. This is the right side of the template. You need only one plastic template for each different pattern piece.

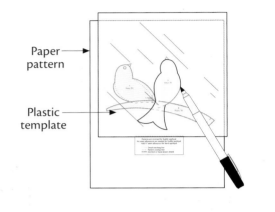

Paper pattern

Plastic template

A Note about the Patterns

The appliqué patterns throughout this book have been drawn in reverse for paper-template appliqué and fusible appliqué. If you are using a hand-appliqué technique, such as needle-turn appliqué, or if you are making a placement guide, you will need to make a reversed, or mirror, image.

To make a plastic template for needle-turn appliqué, simply trace the pattern and then turn your template over and mark that as the right side.

To make a reverse image for a placement guide, trace the entire appliqué pattern onto a piece of paper; then place the paper on a light box or against a bright window, with the traced side toward the light. Trace the shape onto the back of the paper using a black permanent pen.

Appliqué Placement

An easy way to place the appliqué pieces on the block background is to make and use a placement guide underneath the background piece. To make a placement guide, follow the instructions in "A Note about the Patterns" to trace the pattern in reverse onto a piece of paper.

I also like to draw the finished block size around the pattern. This is helpful when the edges of appliqué pieces are sewn into the seam later. Do this by placing a square ruler over the pattern with the midpoint of the block over the center point marked on the pattern. Trace two sides of the ruler, rotate the paper, reposition the ruler, and draw the other two sides (as described in "Squaring Up Blocks" on page 7).

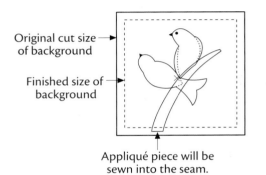

Original cut size of background

Finished size of background

Appliqué piece will be sewn into the seam.

Lay the placement guide on a table or your ironing board, and lay the background fabric over it. Carefully match the center marks and pin in place. Position the appliqués on the background, following the numerical order marked on the pattern.

If you find it difficult to see your design through the background fabric, you can use a light box or try using a pattern overlay. A pattern overlay is helpful when the pattern has many layers of appliqué pieces, such as in "Rose and Bow Wreath" on page 37.

To make a pattern overlay, use a permanent marker to trace the pattern onto a piece of clear template plastic or acetate that is the same size as your background piece. Place the plastic over the background fabric, pinning or taping it in place if desired. To position each appliqué piece, lift up the plastic and slide each piece under the appropriate marking. Remove the plastic overlay and then pin, baste, or fuse the appliqué to the background fabric.

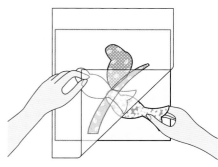

Slide appliqué shapes under the overlay to place them on the background.

Paper-Template Appliqué

Paper-template appliqué uses a paper template as a base to make a smooth, curved edge on an appliqué shape. This method is similar to freezer-paper appliqué, except you use a heavy paper (60-lb. drawing paper or construction paper) instead of freezer paper. Since the paper is heavier, it holds its shape better than freezer paper. I used this technique to make the Butterfly blocks in "Butterfly Garden" on page 48, as well as the Basket blocks in "Colonial Scrap Baskets" on page 69 and "Fandango" on page 76. With this method you can prepare all the pieces for the block and preview them before stitching. The pieces can then be stitched by hand or machine.

1. Make plastic templates of each appliqué piece, referring to "Making Appliqué Templates" on page 7. Place each template right side up on a piece of heavy paper. Trace around the template using a pencil or a black permanent pen. Trace each shape the number of times indicated on the pattern.

Multiple Layers

You can cut multiple layers of paper templates for repeated pieces by stapling two or three layers of paper together. First trace the design onto the top layer, and then staple the layers together. The staples will hold the layers together as you cut accurate templates.

2. Cut out the paper templates on the traced line so that they are the exact size of the pattern piece. Draw a mark to indicate the right side of the template. Use ½" appliqué pins to pin each paper template right side up on the wrong side of the chosen fabric. Cut out the shape, adding a ³⁄₁₆"-wide seam allowance all around. Then use one of the methods described below to appliqué the shape to the background fabric.

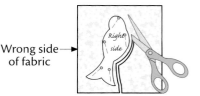

Wrong side of fabric

Hand Appliqué

1. Use your fingers to turn and hand baste the seam allowance over the paper template, using a light color of thread in your needle and removing the pins as you come to them. Clip any curves or inside points as needed.

2. Follow the appliqué pattern or placement guide to position piece 1 on the background fabric. Pin or baste the appliqué in place.

3. Thread an appliqué needle with a thread color that matches the appliqué fabric. Use a traditional appliqué stitch to sew the piece to the background.

4. When the appliqué piece is completely stitched in place, remove the basting stitches. Carefully cut a slit in the background fabric behind the appliqué shape and remove the paper template. (If you will be hand quilting, you may want to cut away the excess background fabric behind the appliqué shape, leaving a ¼" seam allowance.)

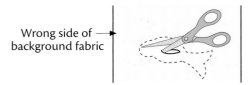

Wrong side of background fabric

5. Repeat steps 2–4 to position and appliqué the remaining pieces in numerical order. When all the appliqué is complete, gently press and square up the block, referring to "Squaring Up Blocks" on page 7.

Machine Appliqué

For this method, spray starch takes the place of hand basting. Using starch saves time when preparing the pieces for appliqué, and unlike a glue stick, starch doesn't require that you soak the fabrics in water to remove the adhesive. You will need a can of spray starch, a small cup, and a ⅜" stencil brush or small paintbrush (I prefer white bristles).

1. After cutting out each appliqué shape as described in "Paper-Template Appliqué" on page 9, remove the pins. Spray a small amount of starch into a cup. (I start with a small amount and replenish as needed.)

Heat-Resistant Template Plastic

When using spray starch, you may want to use a heat-resistant template plastic, such as Templar, instead of the heavy paper. To do this, make heat-resistant plastic templates of each appliqué piece, referring to "Making Appliqué Templates" on page 7. Then follow step 2 in "Paper-Template Appliqué" on page 9 using the plastic template to cut out each appliqué shape; use double-sided tape instead of pins. You can reuse the plastic template or make several of the same shape, if desired.

2. Place the appliqué shape flat, with the wrong side up, on your ironing board. Dip the brush in the starch and "paint" the starch over the seam allowance of the shape. Do not paint the edge that will lie under another piece, because that edge will not need to be basted. Wait a few minutes for the starch to penetrate the fabric. You can paint another shape and then go back to the first shape.

3. Center the paper template, right side up, on the wrong side of the appliqué fabric shape. Using the paper template as a guide and with a dry iron, press the seam allowance over the edge of the paper. Clip the seam allowances on inside curves and inside points to within one or two threads from the paper, as you come to them. On outside curves, once you've achieved a smooth edge, flatten the seam allowance into little pleats or clip the seam allowance so the fabric overlaps.

Pressing Tip

To keep from burning your fingers, use the pointed end of a 6" bamboo skewer or a wooden orange stick to manipulate the fabric around points and curves, as well as to hold the seam allowance in place while ironing.

Bamboo skewer

4. For leaves and other pieces with outside points, fold one edge of the fabric leaf over the template, extending the fold beyond the points of the paper on each end. Fold the other side in the same way. The leaf will have smooth curves and sharp points, with little fabric "flags" sticking out at each end. Fold the flags behind each point and press with your iron. There will probably be enough starch to

hold the flags in place. If not, apply a small amount and press again.

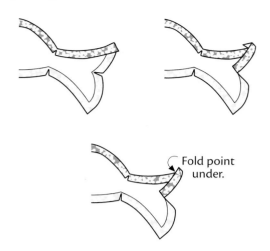

Fold point under.

5. Allow the piece to cool; then remove the paper template and press again if needed. Stitch the appliqué pieces to the block background using the invisible machine appliqué stitch described below. When the appliqué is complete, gently press and square up the block, referring to "Squaring Up Blocks" on page 7.

Invisible Machine Appliqué

For this method, I like to use a very small machine blanket stitch, or you can use the blind hem stitch on your machine. You will need to adjust the length and width of the stitches to use this method effectively. When done well, it is difficult to tell the results from hand appliqué.

1. Prepare the appliqué pieces as instructed in "Machine Appliqué" on page 10.

2. Thread the top of your machine with invisible nylon thread (size .004). Thread the bobbin with a fine thread (60-weight) that matches the background fabric or, depending on your machine, you may want to try using invisible thread in your bobbin. When threading the bobbin with regular thread, bring the thread through the hole in the "finger" on the bobbin (if your machine has one) to slightly increase the bobbin tension. Reduce the top tension. Use a fine needle, size 60/8.

3. Use an open-toe embroidery presser foot and set the machine to the blanket stitch or blind hem stitch. Shorten the stitch length so that the distance the machine sews straight (between the stitches that swing to the left) is about ⅛". Adjust the stitch width so that the needle swings to the left no more than ¹⁄₁₆".

4. Make a test piece with fabric scraps to check your stitch. Sew along the edge of a piece of folded fabric so that the straight stitches are in the background fabric, very close to the folded edge, and the swing stitch just catches the edge of the folded piece. The bobbin thread should not show on the top. Readjust the machine as necessary to achieve the proper stitch.

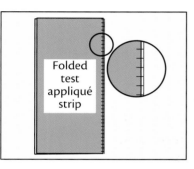

Folded test appliqué strip

5. Pin or use a little fabric glue to hold the piece in place on the block background. Position and appliqué the pieces in numerical order. Sew slowly, turning and pivoting the block as needed. Make sure the points are secured by a swing stitch on each side. Secure the thread ends by backstitching a few stitches. (The backstitches will not show on the front because of the invisible thread.)

Fabric Glue

A variety of fabric-basting glues and glue sticks are available. Whichever one you choose, make sure it will wash out after the project is done. My favorite is Roxanne's Glue-Baste-It, which comes in a little plastic bottle and has a long, pointed nozzle.

Fusible Appliqué

Fusible appliqué is extra fast and easy. With this technique, there are no seam allowances to turn under, so it's a good method to use for appliqué patterns with sharp points, such as "Peony Garden" on page 63. I like to use a decorative stitch such as a machine blanket stitch or zigzag stitch to secure the edges of the appliqué pieces. The decorative stitch adds texture, depth, and color to the project. You can use thread that matches the appliqué pieces or use a contrasting thread. I use a 60-weight, 100%-cotton thread. Use an open-toe embroidery foot so you can see the stitching line clearly.

Fusible web is available with smooth paper on one side and an adhesive on the reverse, or with paper on both sides and an adhesive in the middle. There are many brands on the market, but I prefer Lite Steam-A-Seam or Lite Steam-A-Seam 2. When you purchase a fusible-web product, take time to read the manufacturer's directions. Different products call for different heat settings and handling instructions. Be careful not to allow your hot iron to directly touch fusible web that is not covered by paper or fabric. I recommend using an appliqué pressing sheet or parchment paper to protect your iron; place it on top of the fabric or appliqué pieces when fusing.

1. Make a plastic template for each appliqué shape as described in "Making Appliqué Templates" on page 7. Place each template on the paper side of the fusible web *right side up* and trace around it. Use a pencil or permanent marker to trace each shape the number of times indicated on the pattern, leaving about ½" between shapes. To make a reverse image, turn the template over so that its right side is *down* (next to the paper), and trace the number of reverse shapes indicated on the pattern.

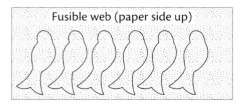
Fusible web (paper side up)

2. Roughly cut the shape out of the fusible web, leaving about ¼" margin all around the marked line.

For larger pieces, or where pieces will be layered, cut out the center of the fusible-web shapes. Leave at least ¼" inside the line. This trimming allows the shape to adhere to the background while eliminating the stiffness within the shape.

Cut approximately ¼" outside the line.   Cut approximately ¼" inside the line.

3. Place the shape, fusible-web side down, on the wrong side of the appropriate appliqué fabric. Following the manufacturer's directions, iron in place. Let cool before handling.

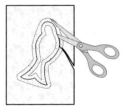

4. Cut out the fabric shape on the drawn line and remove the paper backing.

Removing the Paper

If you haven't cut away the center of the fusible web, try this tip. After cutting out the fabric shape along the drawn line, use a pin to score the paper in the center of the shape. Fold the shape along the scored line to loosen the paper and then remove it from the fabric.

5. Using your pattern as a guide, position the appliqué shape, adhesive side down, on the right side of the background fabric and press.

6. When all the pieces are fused, finish the edges with a decorative stitch, such as a machine blanket stitch. Sew so that the straight stitches are in the background fabric, very close to the appliqué edge, and the swing stitch is in the appliqué piece. You can also use a narrow zigzag stitch on the edges of the appliqué.

Blanket stitch

Zigzag stitch

EMBELLISHMENT

Some of the appliqué patterns include embellishments, which, of course, are optional or can be done using different methods. The line details can be drawn with a permanent pen. I like a Pigma Micron pen because it makes a fine line that doesn't bleed into the fabric background. To draw a line, use the appliqué pattern and a light box or other light source. Start by tracing the line lightly, and then go back over the line several times until you have achieved the desired look.

If you prefer to machine stitch or hand embroider the block details, use the appliqué pattern and a light box (or other light source) and lightly trace the line. If I'm using black thread, I use a permanent marker or fine-point mechanical pencil; however, if I'm using a thread color that matches the appliqué pieces, I use a blue water-soluble marker. Before pressing, just be sure to spray the blue lines with water so they disappear. To machine stitch the line detail, use a short, straight stitch and 50-weight thread. To hand embroider details, follow the stitching instructions below.

Stem Stitch

Bring the needle up at A and down at B. Repeat, bringing the needle up at C and down at D. Continue, keeping the thread on the same side of the stitching line.

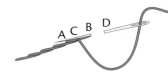

French Knot

Bring the needle up at A. Wrap the thread around the needle three times. Tighten the wrapped thread and hold the tension with your thumb as you insert the needle back down at B, very close to A. Pull tight to create the knot.

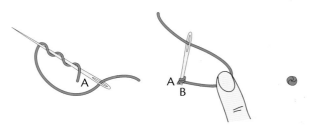

Buttons

To add buttons or beads to your quilt for animal eyes, sew them on in the traditional manner. If the buttons are going to be flower centers, you can attach them in the traditional way or you might want to tie them on using six-strand embroidery floss; if so, tie them so that the thread tails are on the top of the button.

To tie the button on, push the needle down through the buttonhole, leaving a 2" to 3" tail. Bring the needle back up through the opposite buttonhole and cut the thread 2" to 3" above the button. Tie the thread tail in a square knot to secure the button. Trim the thread so it is ¼" to ½" long.

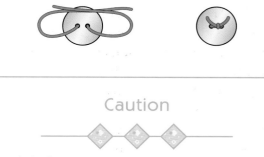

Caution

Refrain from using buttons or beads on quilts intended for infants or toddlers. These small pieces could be a choking hazard.

ASSEMBLING THE QUILT TOP

After you have made all the blocks, cut or made the sashing, and cut setting pieces as needed, you are ready to assemble the quilt top as directed for the project.

❖ QUILTS WITH SASHING STRIPS

For quilts with sashing strips or units, measure the blocks (including seam allowances) and trim the sashing units as needed to match the block measurement. Follow the assembly diagrams for your project to arrange the blocks, sashing strips, and corner squares, if applicable. Join the blocks and vertical sashing strips into rows, pressing the seam allowances toward the sashing strips. Join the horizontal sashing strips and corner squares into rows, once again pressing toward the sashing strips. Sew the rows together and press the seam allowances toward the sashing unit/corner square rows.

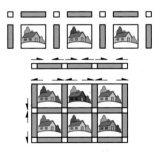

Some quilts are made without corner squares. In that case, the blocks in each horizontal row are separated by vertical sashing strips, and the rows of blocks are separated by long horizontal sashing strips. Measure the completed block rows and trim the long sashing strips to match that measurement.

When the block rows and long sashing strips are sewn together, it's important for the short vertical sashing strips to correctly line up on each side of the long sashing strip. One easy way to achieve this is to mark the long strips with pins to show the junctions that must match. Sew the rows together, matching the seam

junctions with the pins. Press the seam allowances toward the long sashing strips.

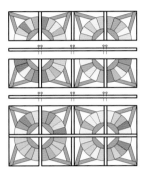

❖ QUILTS SET DIAGONALLY

The blocks for diagonal settings are placed on point and arranged in diagonal rows. Setting triangles are then added to fill in the side and corner spaces.

1. Arrange the blocks, sashing units (if applicable), setting triangles, and corner triangles as shown in the quilt assembly diagram for your project.

2. Sew the blocks, sashing units (if applicable), and side setting triangles together into diagonal rows; press the seam allowances toward the sashing units or toward alternate plain blocks.

3. Sew the rows together, matching the seams from row to row. Press as directed in the project instructions. Sew the corner triangles on last and press the seam allowances toward the corners.

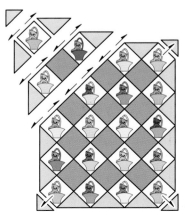

❊ BORDERS

Many quilts from the 1930s are borderless because they were made from scraps, and yardage was scarce. Today, most quilts have a border or borders that frame the pieced blocks. Borders can be simple strips of one or more fabrics. They can also be pieced or appliquéd and used in combination with plain strips.

Prepare border strips a few inches longer than you will actually need; then trim them to the correct length once you know the dimensions of the center of your quilt top. To find the correct measurement for the border strips, always measure through the center of the quilt, not at the outside edges. This ensures that the borders are of equal length on opposite sides of the quilt and helps keep your quilt square.

For borders wider than 2", I usually cut the strips on the lengthwise grain (parallel to the selvage) so that they don't stretch and don't have to be pieced. You'll save fabric if you attach the border strips to the longer sides first and then to the remaining two sides.

For quilts smaller than 40" square, or if you do not have enough fabric to cut the strips from the lengthwise grain, strips cut on the crosswise grain (across the fabric from selvage to selvage) work perfectly fine.

Borders less than 2" wide are usually cut from the crosswise grain and joined end to end with a diagonal seam to achieve the required length. This is the most fabric-efficient way to cut narrow border strips.

Measuring for Borders

1. Measure the length of the quilt top from top to bottom through the center. Cut two border strips to this measurement, piecing as necessary.

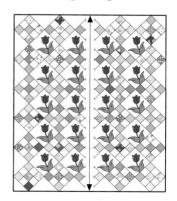

Measure the center of the quilt, top to bottom.

2. Mark the center of the border strips and the center of the sides of the quilt top. Pin the borders to the sides of the quilt top, matching centers and ends. Ease or slightly stretch the quilt top to fit the border strip as necessary. Sew the side borders in place with a ¼" seam allowance and press the seam allowances toward the border strips.

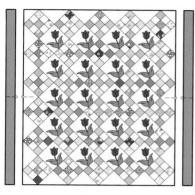

Mark centers.

3. Measure the width of the quilt top from side to side through the center (including the side borders just added) to determine the length of the top and bottom border strips. Cut two strips to this measurement, piecing as necessary. Mark the center of the border strips and the center of the top and bottom of the quilt top. Pin the borders to the quilt top, matching centers and ends. Ease or slightly stretch the quilt to fit the border strips as necessary. Sew the borders in place with a ¼" seam allowance and press the seam allowances toward the border strip.

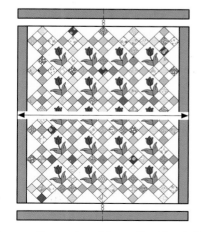

Measure the center of the quilt, side to side, including the borders. Mark centers.

15

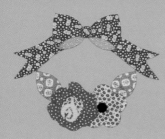

FINISHING TECHNIQUES

A quilt consists of three layers—the quilt top, backing, and batting. Once your quilt top is done, you are ready to move on to the finishing stages.

BACKING AND BATTING

For the quilt backing, cut a piece of fabric 4" to 6" larger than the quilt top (2" to 3" on all sides). For quilts wider than the width of your fabric, you'll need to piece the backing. For most quilts in this book, I've listed enough backing fabric to piece the backing with one seam, leaving enough leftover fabric to cut a hanging sleeve, if desired. When piecing the backing, be sure to trim off the selvages before sewing the pieces together. Press the seam open to reduce bulk.

There are many types of batting to choose from. The type you select will depend on whether you plan to hand or machine quilt your quilt top. Generally, the thinner the batting—whether cotton or polyester—the easier it is to hand quilt. For machine quilting, a cotton batting works best. It won't move or slip between the quilt top and backing. Whatever type of batting you choose, the piece should be large enough to allow an extra 2" around all edges of the quilt top.

LAYERING AND QUILTING YOUR QUILT

Before you layer the quilt, give the quilt top and backing a careful pressing. Then spread the backing, wrong side up, on a flat, clean surface. Anchor the backing with pins or masking tape, taking care not to stretch the fabric out of shape. Center the batting over the backing, smoothing out any wrinkles. Center the pressed quilt top, right side up, over the batting, smoothing out any wrinkles and making sure the edges of the quilt top are parallel to the edges of the backing. Note that you should always smooth outward from the center and along straight lines to ensure that the blocks and borders remain straight.

Pieced Batting

We all have leftover pieces of batting; here's an easy way to put them to use. To join two pieces of batting, place them on a flat surface, overlapping them by 4" to 6". Use utility scissors to cut the overlapped edges in a wavy line. Remove the "waste" pieces and carefully reposition the batting pieces, nestling together—but not overlapping—the curved edges. Use a needle and thread to stitch the pieces together with a large herringbone stitch or cross-stitch.

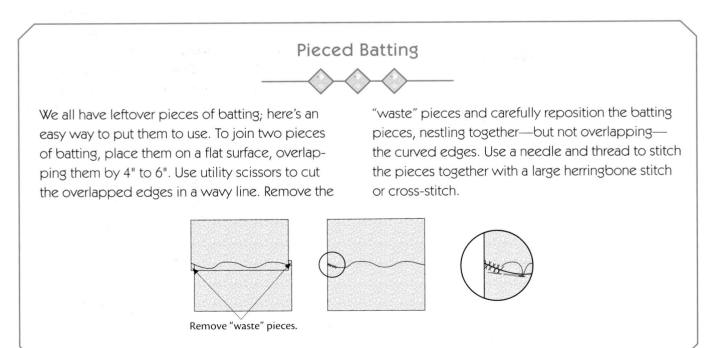

Remove "waste" pieces.

For hand quilting, baste with needle and thread, starting in the center of the quilt and working diagonally to each corner. Continue basting in a grid of horizontal and vertical lines 6" to 8" apart. To finish, baste around the edges about ⅛" from the edge of the quilt top.

For machine quilting, baste the layers with size #2 rustproof safety pins. Place pins 4" to 6" apart; try to avoid areas where you intend to quilt. Finish by machine basting around the edges about ⅛" from the edge of the quilt top.

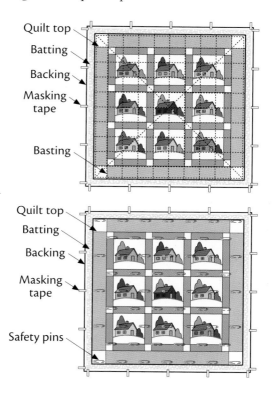

As a general rule, no unquilted areas should exceed 4" x 4". In addition, check the package of the batting that you are using for recommendations concerning the appropriate amount of quilting. The density of quilting should be similar throughout the entire quilt so that the quilt will remain square and not become distorted.

The quilts in this book are all quilted by machine, which is suitable for any type and size of quilt and allows you to complete a project quickly. For straight-line quilting, it is extremely helpful to have a walking foot to evenly feed the layers through the machine without shifting or puckering. For free-motion quilting, you need a darning foot and the ability to drop the feed dogs on your machine. With free-motion quilting, you don't turn the fabric under the needle but instead guide the fabric in the direction of the design. Because the feed dogs are lowered, the stitch length is determined by the speed at which you run the machine and feed the fabric under the foot. For more information on machine quilting, refer to *Machine Quilting Made Easy!* by Maurine Noble (Martingale & Company, 1994).

Walking foot attachment   Darning foot

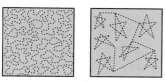

Free-motion quilting designs

▣ SQUARING UP YOUR QUILT

When you complete the quilting, you'll need to trim the excess backing and batting as well as square up your quilt before sewing on the binding. Make sure all the basting threads or pins have been removed, but leave the basting stitches around the outer edges. Align a ruler with the seam line of the outer border and measure the width of the outer border in several places. Using the narrowest measurement, position a ruler along the seam line of the outer border, and trim the excess batting and backing from all four sides. Use a large, square ruler to square up each corner.

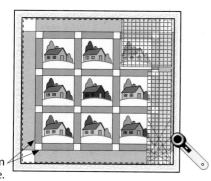

Use these seam lines as a guide.

◼ MAKING A HANGING SLEEVE

If you plan to hang the finished quilt, attach a hanging sleeve or rod pocket to the back now, before you bind the quilt.

From the leftover backing fabric, cut an 8"-wide strip of fabric equal to the width of your quilt. On each short end of the strip, fold over ½", and then fold ½" again to make a hem. Press and stitch by machine.

Fold the strip in half lengthwise, wrong sides together; baste the raw edges to the top edge of the back of your quilt. These raw edges will be secured when you sew on the binding. Your quilt should be about 1" wider than the sleeve on both sides.

Make a little pleat in the sleeve to accommodate the thickness of the rod, and then slip-stitch the ends and bottom edge of the sleeve to the backing fabric. This keeps the rod from being inserted next to the quilt backing.

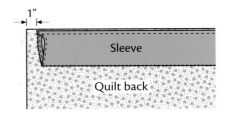

◼ BINDING YOUR QUILT

The binding is a wonderful opportunity to add to the overall look of your quilt. If you want the binding to "disappear," then use the same fabric for the binding as for the outer border. If you prefer the binding to frame the outer border or act as an additional border, then use a fabric that is different from the outer border.

Strips for binding are generally cut 2" to 2½" wide, depending on your preference for binding width and your choice of batting. (I used 2"-wide strips for the quilts in this book.) Cut enough strips to go around the perimeter of your quilt plus about 10" extra for making seams and turning corners.

1. To make one long, continuous strip, piece the strips at right angles and stitch across the corner as shown. Trim the excess fabric, leaving a ¼"-wide seam, and press the seam allowance open.

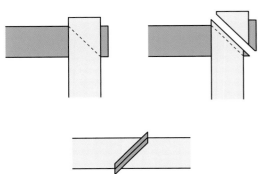

2. Cut one end of the long binding strip at a 45° angle. Press the strip in half lengthwise, wrong sides together and raw edges aligned.

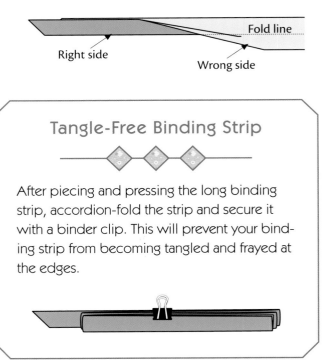

Tangle-Free Binding Strip

After piecing and pressing the long binding strip, accordion-fold the strip and secure it with a binder clip. This will prevent your binding strip from becoming tangled and frayed at the edges.

3. Beginning with the angled end of the binding strip, align the raw edge of the strip with the raw edge of the quilt. Starting on the bottom edge of the quilt (not at a corner), and beginning 8" from the angled end of the strip, use a walking foot and

a ¼"-wide seam to stitch the binding strip to the quilt. Stop ¼" from the first corner and backstitch.

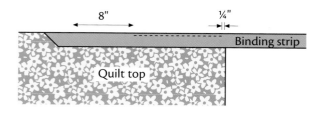

4. Remove the quilt from the sewing machine. Fold the binding straight up and away from the quilt so the fold forms a 45° angle. Fold the binding back down onto itself, even with the edge of the quilt top, and pin as shown to create an angled pleat at the corner. Begin with a backstitch at the fold of the binding and continue stitching along the edge of the quilt top, mitering each corner as you come to it.

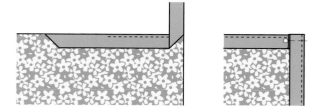

5. Stop stitching approximately 12" from the starting end of the binding strip and backstitch. Remove the quilt from the machine. Place the quilt on a flat surface and layer the beginning (angled) tail on top of the ending tail. Mark the ending tail where it meets the beginning tail. Make a second mark ½" to the right of the first mark.

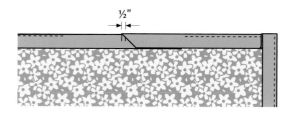

6. Open the ending tail strip and align the 45° line of a small Bias Square with the top edge of the opened binding strip. Place the corner of the ruler on the second mark. Cut the ending tail strip along

the edge of the ruler as shown. The ends of both binding strips will form 45° angles and overlap ½".

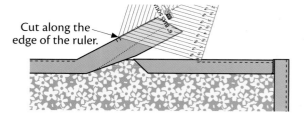

7. Place the binding ends right sides together, aligning the angled raw edges as shown. Fold the quilt out of the way and stitch the ends together using a ¼" seam allowance. Press the seam allowance open, refold the binding, and press the fold. Then finish stitching the binding to the quilt top.

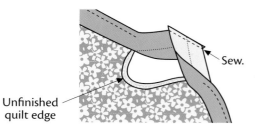

8. Turn the binding to the back of the quilt. Using thread to match the binding, hand stitch the binding in place so that the folded edge covers the row of machine stitching. At each corner, fold the binding to form a miter on the back of the quilt.

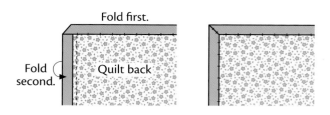

ADDING A LABEL

A label provides important information including the name of the quilt, the person who made it, when it was made, and where. You may also want to include the name of the recipient, if the quilt is a gift, and any other interesting or significant facts about the quilt. A label can be as elaborate or as simple as you desire. You can sign your name on the back of the finished quilt using a permanent marker, purchase pretty labels that are printed on fabric, or make your own label.

BLUEBIRDS AND FRIENDS

Made by Nancy Mahoney. Machine quilted by Karen Housel.

Finished Quilt Size: 50" x 60" ◆ Finished Block Size: 7"

Bluebirds are a symbol of good luck. This darling Alice Brooks design was available from the *Arizona Republic* Household Arts Department for 15 cents in coin. The pattern was described as "a colorful quilt that's easy to make—and one block makes an attractive pillow." I selected bright scraps for the birds and finished them with an outline stitched in charcoal gray thread. The addition of simple pieced blocks—the Autumn Tint design—completes this cheerful quilt.

❈ MATERIALS

Yardages are based on 42"-wide fabrics. Fat eighths measure 9" x 21".

1⅔ yards of pink floral for outer border

1 yard of cream solid for block backgrounds

⅔ yard of dark blue print for inner border and binding

⅝ yard of small-scale floral for Autumn Tint blocks

½ yard of yellow print for setting triangles

1 fat eighth *each* of 10 assorted blue prints for Autumn Tint blocks and bird appliqués

1 fat eighth *each* of 10 assorted red prints for Autumn Tint blocks and bird appliqués

1 rectangle, 5" x 8", *each* of 10 assorted green prints for tree branch appliqués

3¼ yards of fabric for backing

55" x 65" piece of batting

2 yards of 16"-wide fusible web (optional)

Black or charcoal gray thread for appliqués and bird details and/or 6-strand embroidery floss for bird details

Black Pigma pen (size 05) for beak and eye details

❈ CUTTING

All measurements include ¼"-wide seam allowances. Cut all strips across the width of fabric unless otherwise indicated.

From the cream solid, cut:

◆ 4 strips, 8" x 42"; crosscut into 20 squares, 8" x 8"

From *each* of the 10 assorted blue prints, cut:

◆ 6 squares, 2¼" x 2¼" (60 total)

From *each* of the 10 assorted red prints, cut:

◆ 6 squares, 2¼" x 2¼" (60 total)

From the small-scale floral, cut:

◆ 4 strips, 4" x 42"; crosscut into 32 squares, 4" x 4"

From the yellow print, cut:

◆ 7 squares, 6¼" x 6¼"; cut twice diagonally to yield 28 triangles

◆ 2 squares, 5⅞" x 5⅞"; cut once diagonally to yield 4 triangles

From the dark blue print, cut:

◆ 5 inner-border strips, 1½" x 42"

◆ 6 binding strips, 2" x 42"

From the *lengthwise* grain of the pink floral, cut:

◆ 4 strips, 4½" x 55"

APPLIQUÉING THE BLOCKS

1. Choose your favorite appliqué method and make appliqué templates for the birds and tree branch by tracing the patterns on page 24. Refer to "Appliqué Techniques" on page 7 for details as needed. Make the quantity indicated on the pattern for each shape. Refer to the photo on page 20 for color-placement guidance.

2. Using the pattern as a placement guide, position the birds and tree branches on the 8" cream squares. Be sure the cream squares are positioned on point. Appliqué the pieces in numerical order as indicated on the pattern. Use the black Pigma pen to add the beak and eye details. To add the stitching-line details, use a straight stitch on your machine or embroider a stem stitch by hand.

3. Make 20 appliqué blocks. Gently press and then trim each block to 7½" x 7½", referring to "Squaring Up Blocks" on page 7.

7½"   7½"

Make 20.

MAKING THE AUTUMN TINT BLOCKS

1. Randomly sew the 2¼" assorted blue squares and assorted red squares together in pairs as shown. Press the seam allowances toward the blue squares. Make 60 units. Sew two units together as shown to make a four-patch unit; press. Make 30 four-patch units.

Make 60.

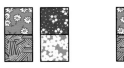

Make 30.

2. Sew two four-patch units and two 4" floral squares into rows as shown. Sew the rows together to make one block; press. Make 12 Autumn Tint blocks. (You'll have six four-patch units left over to use in step 1 of "Making the Setting Triangles.")

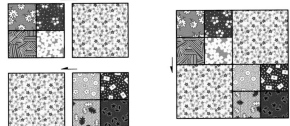

Make 12.

MAKING THE SETTING TRIANGLES

1. To make the top and bottom setting triangles, sew one four-patch unit and two 6¼" yellow triangles together as shown. Press the seam allowances toward the yellow triangles. Make six four-patch triangle units.

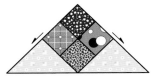

Make 6.

2. To make the side setting triangles, sew one 4" floral print square and two 6¼" yellow triangles together as shown. Press the seam allowances toward the yellow triangles. Make eight side triangles.

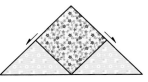

Make 8.

QUILT-TOP ASSEMBLY

For detailed instructions, refer to "Quilts Set Diagonally" on page 14.

1. Referring to the quilt assembly diagram, arrange the appliqué blocks, Autumn Tint blocks, four-patch triangles, and side triangles in diagonal rows.

2. Sew the pieces in each row together. Press the seam allowances away from the appliquéd blocks. Stitch the rows together; press the seam allowances

in one direction. Add a 5⅞" yellow triangle to each corner.

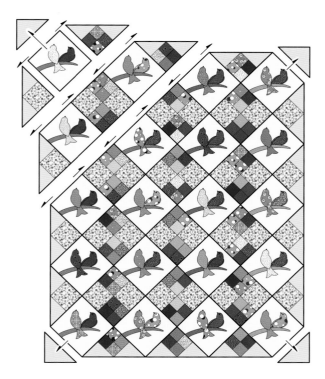

3. Refer to "Borders" on page 15 to measure, cut, and sew the 1½"-wide blue strips for the inner border and then the 4½"-wide pink floral strips for the outer border. Press all seam allowances toward the newly added border strips.

❖ FINISHING THE QUILT

Referring to "Finishing Techniques" on page 16, cut and piece the backing fabric and then layer the quilt top with batting and backing. After basting the layers together, hand or machine quilt as desired; see the quilting suggestions below. Trim the batting and backing so that the edges are even with the quilt top. Using the 2"-wide blue strips, sew the binding to the quilt.

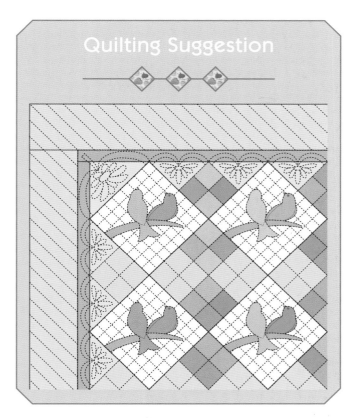

Quilting Suggestion

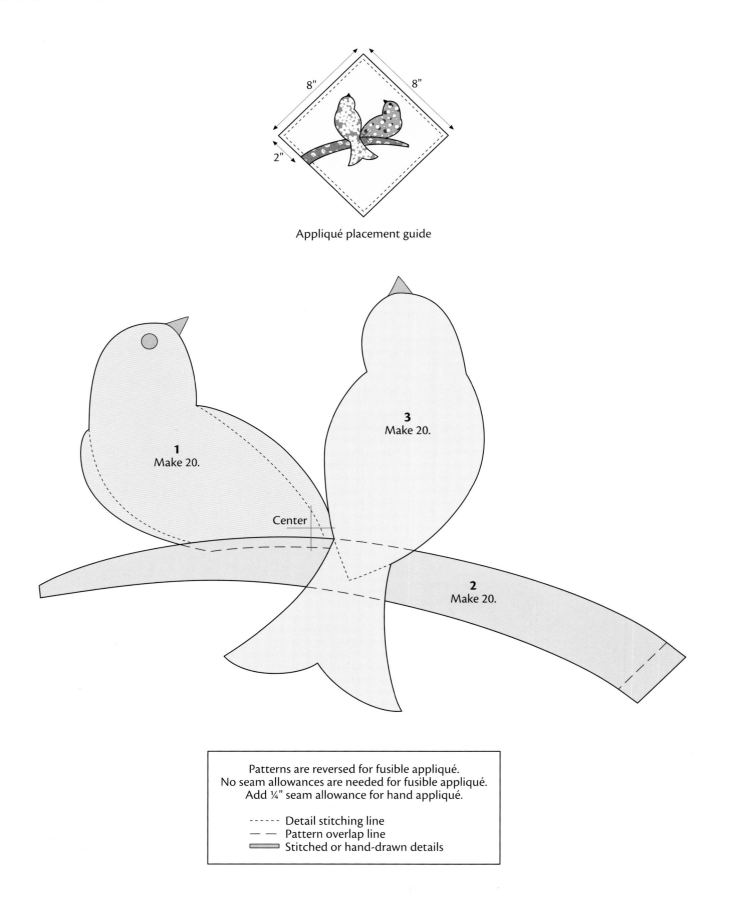

Appliqué placement guide

8"

8"

2"

1
Make 20.

3
Make 20.

Center

2
Make 20.

Patterns are reversed for fusible appliqué.
No seam allowances are needed for fusible appliqué.
Add ¼" seam allowance for hand appliqué.

- - - - - Detail stitching line
— — Pattern overlap line
▭ Stitched or hand-drawn details

FLOWER GARDEN

Made by Nancy Mahoney. Machine quilted by Nannette Moore.

Finished Quilt Size: 46½" x 55¾" ◆ Finished Block Size: 8"

The *Arizona Republic* newspaper enticed readers with the following description of this Alice Brooks design: "Practical—and pretty, too—is this scrap quilt design. The perky flowerpot appliqués that decorate each block may be done in a variety of print fabrics to use your scraps." As suggested, I used scraps for the flower and leaf appliqués, and added rickrack stems and button flower centers. This delightful quilt will bring a welcome touch of spring to any room.

▨ MATERIALS

Yardages are based on 42"-wide fabrics. Fat eighths measure 9" x 21".

1¼ yards of dark aqua print for outer border and binding

1¼ yards of aqua-and-cream print for sashing and setting triangles

⅞ yard of cream solid for block backgrounds

⅓ yard of yellow print for inner border

1 fat eighth of brown print for flowerpot appliqués

1 rectangle, 3" x 6", *each* of 11 assorted green prints for leaf appliqués

1 square, 4" x 4", *each* of 22 assorted red, pink, orchid, peach, yellow, orange, and blue prints for flower appliqués

3¼ yards of fabric for backing

52" x 61" piece of batting

1⅓ yards of 16"-wide fusible web (optional)

1¾ yards of green baby rickrack (¼") for stems

22 yellow buttons (about ½" diameter) for flower centers

Thread in coordinating colors for appliqués and flower details and/or 6-strand embroidery floss for flower details

Yellow 6-strand embroidery floss for buttons

▨ CUTTING

All measurements include ¼"-wide seam allowances. Cut all strips across the width of fabric unless otherwise indicated.

From the cream solid, cut:

◆ 3 strips, 9" x 42"; crosscut into 11 squares, 9" x 9"

From the aqua-and-cream print, cut:

◆ 3 strips, 1½" x 42"

◆ 6 squares, 12¾" x 12¾"; cut twice diagonally to yield 24 triangles. (You'll have 2 extra triangles.)

◆ 4 squares, 6¾" x 6¾"; cut once diagonally to yield 8 triangles

From the yellow print, cut:

◆ 5 strips, 1½" x 42"

From the dark aqua print, cut:

◆ 6 strips, 4½" x 42"

◆ 6 strips, 2" x 42"

✿ APPLIQUÉING THE BLOCKS

1. Choose your favorite appliqué method and make appliqué templates for the flowers, leaves, and flowerpots by tracing the patterns on pages 30 and 31. Refer to "Appliqué Techniques" on page 7 for details as needed. Make the quantity indicated on the pattern for each shape. Refer to the photo on page 25 for color-placement ideas. I made six blocks containing flowers with pointed petals and five blocks with round petals. Make as many of each as you wish, for a total of 22 flowers.

2. From the green rickrack, cut 11 pieces that are 2½" long, 11 pieces that are 2" long, and 11 pieces that are 1" long. Using the pattern as a placement guide and placing the background square on point, use a sharp or mechanical pencil to lightly mark the stem line. Sew the rickrack to the 9" cream squares using a straight stitch.

3. Appliqué the flowerpots, leaves, and flowers in numerical order as indicated on the pattern. To add the stitching-line details to the flowers, use a straight stitch on your machine or hand embroider a stem stitch. To stitch the leaf details, adjust the zigzag stitch on your machine to make a satin stitch or hand embroider a satin stitch or stem stitch.

4. Make 11 appliqué blocks. Gently press and then trim each block to 8½" x 8½", referring to "Squaring Up Blocks" on page 7.

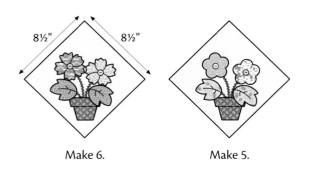

Make 6. Make 5.

✿ QUILT-TOP ASSEMBLY

The setting triangles have been cut slightly oversize. You will trim them after the quilt center is assembled.

1. Assemble and sew four appliqué blocks and six of the aqua-and-cream triangles cut from 12¾" squares into a vertical row as shown; press.

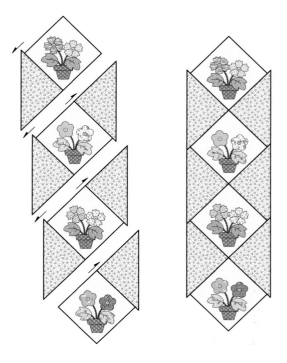

2. Sew four of the aqua-and-cream triangles cut from 6¾" squares to the corners as shown; press. Repeat to make two vertical rows.

Make 2.

3. Assemble and sew three appliqué blocks and 10 of the aqua-and-cream triangles cut from 12¾" squares into one vertical row as shown; press.

Make 1.

4. Square up the two rows with four blocks each by trimming the excess triangle fabrics, leaving a ¼" seam allowance all the way around the pieced strip.

¼" seam allowance

5. Repeat step 4 to trim the long sides of the row with three blocks.

6. Measure the length of the two vertical rows from step 4. If they differ, calculate the average and consider this the length. Trim the top and bottom of the row with three blocks so that its length equals this measurement.

7. Sew the three 1½" x 42" aqua-and-cream strips together end to end to make one continuous strip. From this long strip, cut two sashing strips the length of your measurement from step 6.

8. Sew the block rows and the two sashing strips together as shown. Press the seam allowances toward the sashing strips.

9. Refer to "Borders" on page 15 to measure, cut, and sew the 1½"-wide yellow strips for the inner border and then the 4½"-wide aqua strips for the outer border. Press all seam allowances toward the newly added border strips.

Quilt assembly

FINISHING THE QUILT

Referring to "Finishing Techniques" on page 16, cut and piece the backing fabric and then layer the quilt top with batting and backing. After basting the layers together, hand or machine quilt as desired; see the quilting suggestion below. Trim the batting and backing so that the edges are even with the quilt top. Using the 2"-wide aqua strips, sew the binding to the quilt. Sew a button in the center of each flower using embroidery floss.

Quilting Suggestion

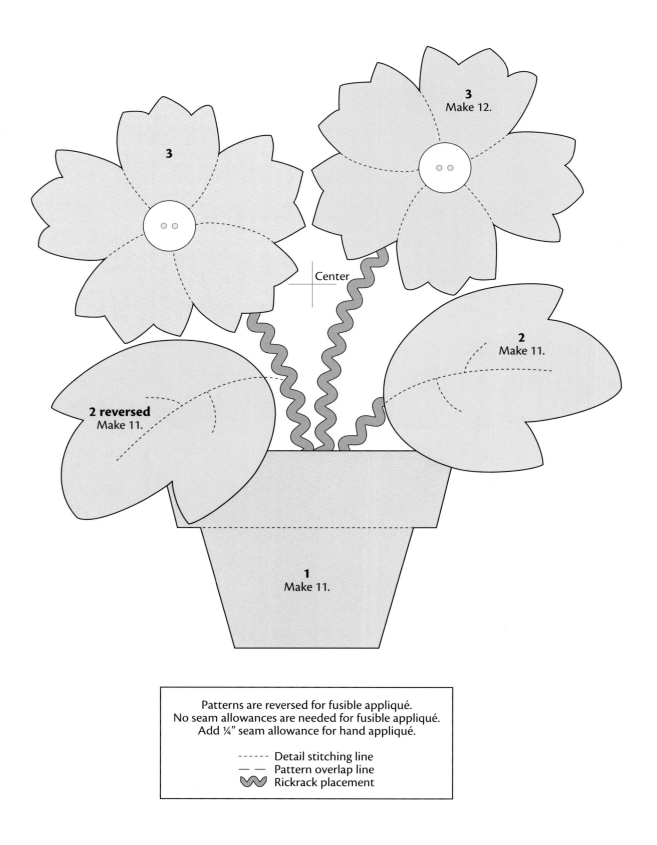

3

3
Make 12.

Center

2
Make 11.

2 reversed
Make 11.

1
Make 11.

Patterns are reversed for fusible appliqué.
No seam allowances are needed for fusible appliqué.
Add ¼" seam allowance for hand appliqué.

------ Detail stitching line
— — Pattern overlap line
〰 Rickrack placement

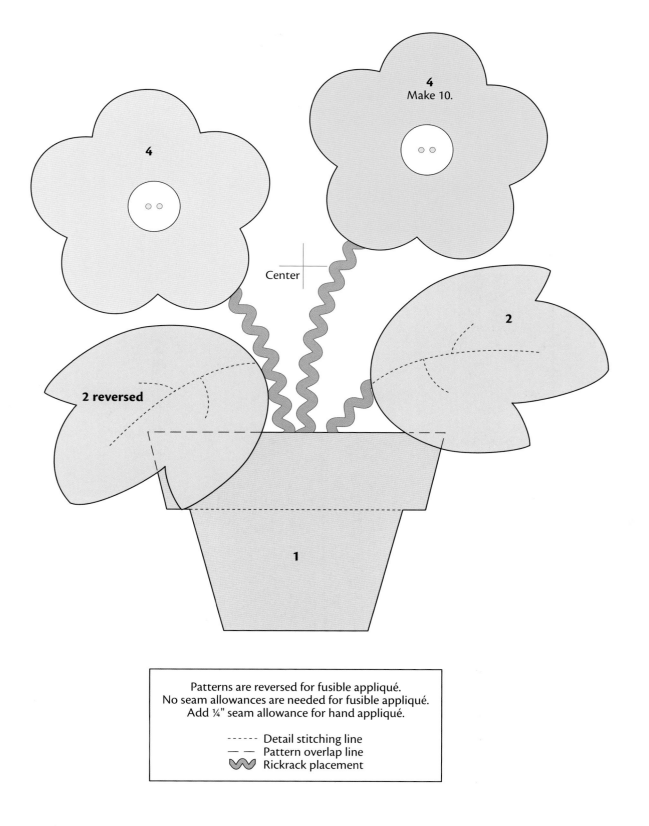

Patterns are reversed for fusible appliqué.
No seam allowances are needed for fusible appliqué.
Add ¼" seam allowance for hand appliqué.

------- Detail stitching line
— — Pattern overlap line
〜〜 Rickrack placement

BUNNY HOP

Made by Nancy Mahoney. Machine quilted by Dawn Kelly.

Finished Quilt Size: 48½" x 67½" ◆ Finished Block Size: 7" x 9"

When published in the *Phoenix Gazette*, this Laura Wheeler design declared: "Hello! says Bunny. And he'd just love to be appliquéd on a nice soft quilt! Use up your scraps and you'll have a quilt to delight any tot." And what a darling bunny he is! I've made the blocks rectangular and added pieced sashing to frame them. The soft color palette makes this crib quilt an ideal choice for your little darling.

 MATERIALS

Yardages are based on 42"-wide fabrics.

2¼ yards of cream solid for block backgrounds and sashing

1¾ yards of peach print for outer border and binding

⅝ yard of small-scale orange print for sashing

1 rectangle, 6" x 8", *each* of 20 assorted peach, purple, blue, yellow, pink, and red prints for bunny appliqués

3⅜ yards of fabric for backing

54" x 73" piece of batting

1¾ yards of 16"-wide fusible web (optional)

Black, red, and green Pigma pens (size 05) for facial details and grass

Black, white, and red thread or 6-strand embroidery floss for facial details

Thread in coordinating colors for appliqués

CUTTING

All measurements include ¼"-wide seam allowances. Cut all strips across the width of fabric unless otherwise indicated.

From the cream solid, cut:

◆ 5 strips, 8" x 42"; crosscut into 20 rectangles, 8" x 10"

◆ 24 strips, 1¼" x 42"

From the small-scale orange print, cut:

◆ 2 strips, 2½" x 42"; crosscut into 30 squares, 2½" x 2½"

◆ 12 strips, 1" x 42"

From the *lengthwise* grain of the peach print, cut:

◆ 4 border strips, 5½" x 63"

◆ 4 binding strips, 2" x 63"

APPLIQUÉING THE BLOCKS

1. Choose your favorite appliqué method and make appliqué templates for the bunny by tracing the pattern on page 36. Refer to "Appliqué Techniques" on page 7 for details as needed. Make the quantity indicated on the pattern for each shape. Refer to the photo on page 32 for color-placement ideas.

2. Using the pattern as a placement guide, position the bunnies on the 8" x 10" cream rectangles. Appliqué the pieces in numerical order as indicated on the pattern. To add the stitching-line details, use a small zigzag stitch on your machine or hand embroider a stem stitch.

3. For the eyes, trace the shape and fill it in using the black Pigma pen. Then use a darning foot and black thread to fill in the shape. By drawing the shape and filling it in with the black pen, you don't need to completely cover the area with thread. Next, use white thread over the black thread to create a small circle. (Adding a little white to the eyes will bring the bunnies to life.) Using the black pen, trace the nose shape, fill in, and stitch with black thread. Then use the red Pigma pen to trace and fill in the mouth; fill it in with red thread. Use the green Pigma pen to add the grass lines.

4. Make 20 bunny blocks. Gently press and then trim each block to 7½" x 9½", referring to "Squaring Up Blocks" on page 7.

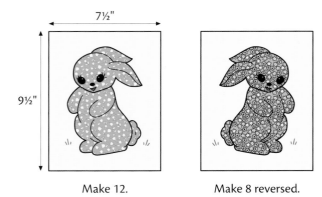

Make 12.   Make 8 reversed.

QUILT-TOP ASSEMBLY

For detailed instructions, refer to "Quilts with Sashing Strips" on page 14.

1. To make the sashing strips, sew a 1¼" x 42" cream strip to both long sides of a 1" x 42" orange strip to make a strip set. Press the seam allowances toward the orange strip. Make a total of 12 strip sets. Cut the strip sets into the number and width of segments indicated.

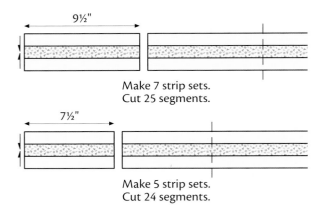

Make 7 strip sets.
Cut 25 segments.

Make 5 strip sets.
Cut 24 segments.

2. Arrange and sew together five 9½" segments from step 1 and four blocks, alternating them as shown to make a block row; press. Make a total of five rows.

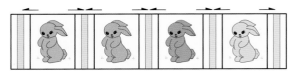

Make 3.

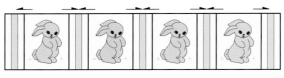

Make 2.

3. Arrange and sew together four 7½" segments from step 1 and five 2½" orange squares as shown to make a sashing row; press. Make six rows.

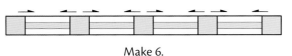

Make 6.

4. Sew the block rows and sashing rows together, alternating them as shown in the quilt assembly diagram. Press the seam allowances toward the sashing rows.

5. Refer to "Borders" on page 15 to measure, cut, and sew the 5½"-wide peach strips for the outer border. Press all seam allowances toward the peach border strips.

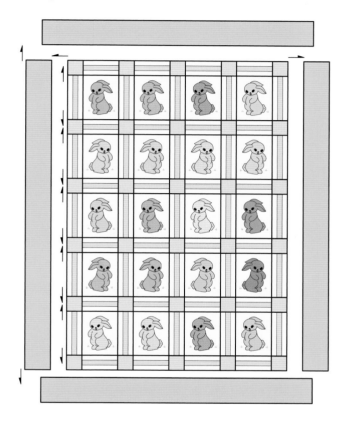

FINISHING THE QUILT

Referring to "Finishing Techniques" on page 16, cut and piece the backing fabric and then layer the quilt top with batting and backing. After basting the layers together, hand or machine quilt as desired; see the quilting suggestion below. Trim the batting and backing so that the edges are even with the quilt top. Using the 2"-wide peach strips, sew the binding to the quilt.

Quilting Suggestion

3
Make 12 and 8 reversed.

Center

2
Make 12 and 8 reversed.

1
Make 12
and 8
reversed.

Patterns are reversed for fusible appliqué.
No seam allowances are needed for fusible appliqué.
Add ¼" seam allowance for hand appliqué.

- - - - - Detail stitching line
— — Pattern overlap line
▭ Stitched or hand-drawn details

ROSE AND BOW WREATH

Designed by Nancy Mahoney, made by Julie Sheckman, and machine quilted by Nannette Moore.

Finished Quilt Size: 60½" x 60½" ◆ Finished Block Size: 10"

The pattern for this lovely wreath block, designed by Alice Brooks, could be ordered from the *Arizona Republic* Household Arts Department. The newspaper's glowing description says it all! "If you want to make your room lovelier, there's no better way of doing it than by making this colorful appliqué quilt. The flowers and bow lend an old-fashioned charm. Do the flowers in various bright print scraps, if you prefer, or you can make the blocks the same throughout." Julie used various red print scraps for the flowers and kept the bow the same throughout. This attractive quilt is sure to brighten your home during the Christmas holidays and all the way through to Valentine's Day.

MATERIALS

Yardages are based on 42"-wide fabrics. Fat eighths measure 9" x 21".

1⅞ yards of dark red print for setting triangles and outer border

1¾ yards of cream solid for block backgrounds

⅞ yard of red-and-cream print for sashing and inner border

½ yard of black solid for binding

½ yard of red floral for bow appliqués

1 fat eighth of pink print for bow appliqués

1 fat eighth *each* of 5 assorted green prints for leaf appliqués

1 fat eighth *each* of 6 assorted red prints for flower appliqués

Scraps of yellow solid and black solid for flower center appliqués

4 yards of fabric for backing

66" x 66" piece of batting

2⅛ yards of 16"-wide fusible web (optional)

Thread or 6-strand embroidery floss in coordinating colors for appliqués and details

CUTTING

All measurements include ¼"-wide seam allowances. Cut all strips across the width of fabric unless otherwise indicated.

From the cream solid, cut:

◆ 5 strips, 11" x 42"; crosscut into 13 squares, 11" x 11"

From the red-and-cream print, cut:

◆ 17 strips, 1½" x 42"; crosscut *9 strips* into:

• 2 strips, 1½" x 34½"

• 2 strips, 1½" x 12½"

• 18 strips, 1½" x 10½"

From the *lengthwise* grain of the dark red print, cut:

◆ 4 strips, 5½" x 65"

◆ 2 squares, 17" x 17"; cut twice diagonally to yield 8 triangles

◆ 2 squares, 9½" x 9½"; cut once diagonally to yield 4 triangles

From the black solid, cut:

◆ 7 strips, 2" x 42"

APPLIQUÉING THE BLOCKS

1. Choose your favorite appliqué method and make appliqué templates for the flowers, flower centers, leaves, and bow by tracing the patterns on pages 41 and 42. Refer to "Appliqué Techniques" on page 7 for details as needed. Make the quantity indicated on the pattern for each shape. Refer to the photo on page 37 for color-placement ideas.

2. Using the pattern as a placement guide, position the flowers, flower centers, leaves, and bows on the 11" cream squares. Appliqué the shapes in numerical order as indicated on the pattern. To add the stitching-line details, use a straight stitch on your machine or hand embroider a stem stitch.

3. Make 13 appliqué blocks. Gently press and then trim each block to 10½" x 10½", referring to "Squaring Up Blocks" on page 7.

10½"   10½"

Make 13.

QUILT-TOP ASSEMBLY

For detailed instructions, refer to "Quilts Set Diagonally" on page 14. The setting triangles have been cut slightly oversize. You will trim them after the quilt center is assembled.

1. Sew three 1½" x 42" red-and-cream strips together end to end to make one continuous strip. From this long strip, cut two sashing strips, 56½" long.

2. Arrange the blocks, the 1½" x 10½" red-and-cream strips, the 1½" x 12½" red-and-cream strips, the 1½" x 34½" red-and-cream strips, and the 56½"-long sashing strips from step 1 in diagonal rows as shown below. Add the red triangles cut from 17" squares to the side edges and the red triangles cut from 9½" squares to the corners.

3. Sew the blocks, the 10½"-long red-and-cream strips, and the side triangles together into rows. Press the seam allowances toward the sashing strips.

4. Sew the block rows and the remaining strips from step 2 together as shown in the quilt assembly diagram. Press the seam allowances toward the sashing strips. Add the corner triangles last.

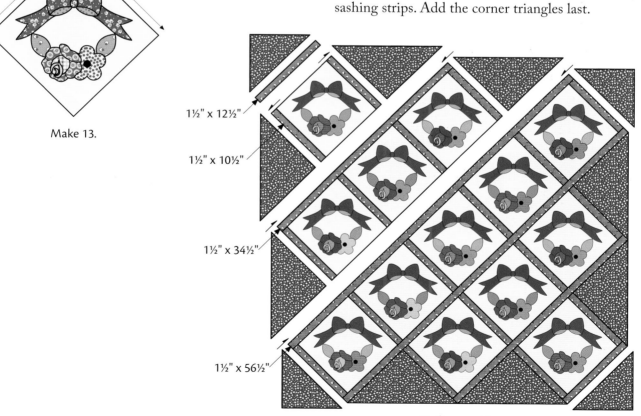

1½" x 12½"

1½" x 10½"

1½" x 34½"

1½" x 56½"

Quilt assembly

5. To trim and straighten the quilt top, align the ¼" mark on your ruler with the outermost points of the sashing. Use a rotary cutter to trim any excess fabric, leaving a ¼"-wide seam allowance. Square the corners of the quilt top as necessary.

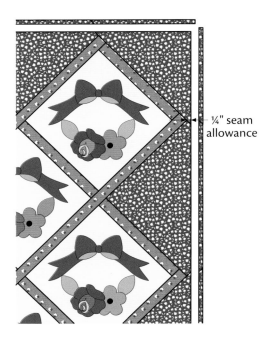

¼" seam allowance

6. Refer to "Borders" on page 15 to measure, cut, and sew the remaining 1½"-wide red-and-cream strips for the inner border and then the 5½"-wide dark red strips for the outer border. Press all seam allowances toward the newly added border strips.

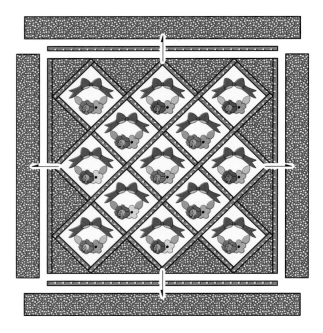

FINISHING THE QUILT

Referring to "Finishing Techniques" on page 16, cut and piece the backing fabric and then layer the quilt top with batting and backing. After basting the layers together, hand or machine quilt as desired; see the quilting suggestion below. Trim the batting and backing so that the edges are even with the quilt top. Using the 2"-wide black strips, sew the binding to the quilt.

Quilting Suggestion

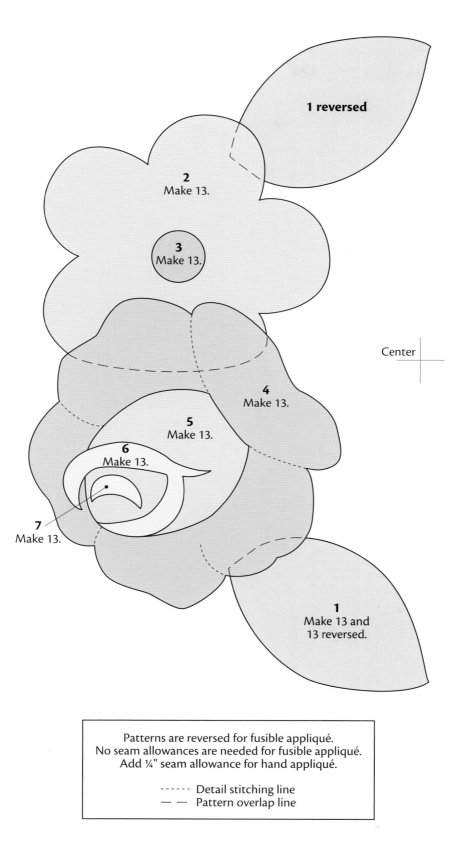

1 reversed

2
Make 13.

3
Make 13.

Center

4
Make 13.

5
Make 13.

6
Make 13.

7
Make 13.

1
Make 13 and
13 reversed.

Patterns are reversed for fusible appliqué.
No seam allowances are needed for fusible appliqué.
Add ¼" seam allowance for hand appliqué.

- - - - - Detail stitching line
— — Pattern overlap line

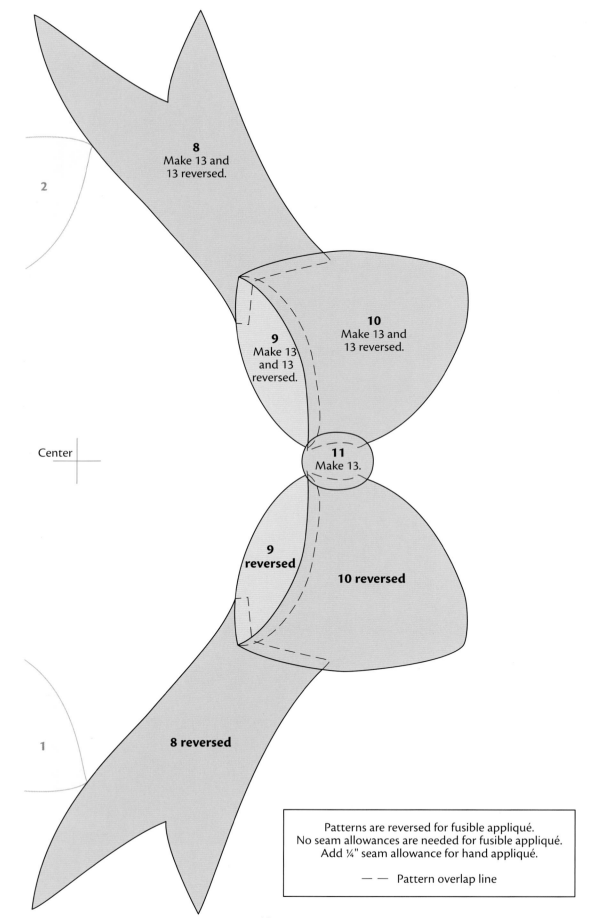

8
Make 13 and
13 reversed.

2

10
Make 13 and
13 reversed.

9
Make 13
and 13
reversed.

Center

11
Make 13.

9
reversed

10 reversed

8 reversed

1

Patterns are reversed for fusible appliqué.
No seam allowances are needed for fusible appliqué.
Add ¼" seam allowance for hand appliqué.

— — Pattern overlap line

42

KITTEN BASKET

Made by Nancy Mahoney. Machine quilted by Karen Housel.

Finished Quilt Size: 71" x 85½" ◆ Finished Block Size: 10"

This winsome Kitten Basket design was published under the Laura Wheeler name. You can use the same prints throughout for the kitten and basket, or use the same fabric for the basket and different fabrics for the kittens. I preferred a scrappy look and used different prints for the kittens and baskets in all the blocks. This quilt is large enough for a twin-size bed and is sure to please anyone who adores kittens.

MATERIALS

Yardages are based on 42"-wide fabrics.

2⅜ yards of cream solid for block backgrounds

2¼ yards of blue star print for outer border and binding

1⅓ yards of light blue floral for setting squares

1 yard of dark blue print for setting triangles

⅜ yard of orange print for inner border

1 rectangle, 7" x 8", *each of 20 assorted light prints—* green, yellow, blue, aqua, orchid, red, brown, and peach—for basket appliqués

1 rectangle, 5" x 6", *each of 20 assorted dark prints—* black, orange, pink, red, aqua, blue, and purple— for kitten appliqués

5⅝ yards of fabric for backing

76" x 91" piece of batting

2¾ yards of 16"-wide fusible web (optional)

Charcoal gray thread for appliqués

Black thread or 6-strand embroidery floss for facial details

Black Pigma pen (size 05) for facial details

CUTTING

All measurements include ¼"-wide seam allowances. Cut all strips across the width of fabric unless otherwise indicated.

From the cream solid, cut:

◆ 7 strips, 11" x 42"; crosscut into 20 squares, 11" x 11"

From the light blue floral, cut:

◆ 4 strips, 10½" x 42"; crosscut into 12 squares, 10½" x 10½"

From the dark blue print, cut:

◆ 4 squares, 15¾" x 15¾"; cut twice diagonally to yield 16 triangles. (You'll have 2 extra triangles.)

◆ 2 squares, 8¼" x 8¼"; cut once diagonally to yield 4 triangles

From the orange print, cut:

◆ 7 strips, 1½" x 42"

From the *lengthwise* grain of the blue star print, cut:

◆ 4 strips, 6½" x 76"

◆ 5 binding strips, 2" x 65"

APPLIQUÉING THE BLOCKS

1. Choose your favorite appliqué method and make appliqué templates for the kitten and basket by tracing the pattern on page 47. Refer to "Appliqué Techniques" on page 7 for details as needed. Make the quantity indicated on the pattern for each shape. Refer to the photo on page 43 for color-placement ideas.

2. Using the pattern as a placement guide, position the kittens and baskets on the 11" cream squares. Be sure the cream squares are positioned on point. Appliqué the pieces in numerical order as indicated on the pattern. To add the stitching-line details, use a straight stitch on your machine or hand embroider a stem stitch.

3. For the eyes, trace the shape and fill in using the black Pigma pen. Then use a darning foot and black thread to fill in the eye shape. By drawing and filling the shape first, you don't need to completely cover the area with thread. Trace the nose shape and fill with black thread.

4. Make 20 appliqué blocks. Gently press and then trim each block to 10½" x 10½", referring to "Squaring Up Blocks" on page 7.

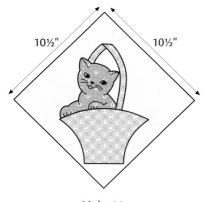

10½"   10½"

Make 20.

QUILT-TOP ASSEMBLY

For detailed instructions, refer to "Quilts Set Diagonally" on page 14. The setting triangles have been cut slightly oversize. You will trim them after the quilt center is assembled.

1. Lay out the Kitten blocks and 10½" light blue setting squares. Add the blue triangles cut from 15¾" squares.

2. Sew the blocks, setting squares, and side triangles together into rows. Press the seam allowances away from the Kitten blocks.

3. Sew the rows together, adding the blue corner triangles cut from 8¼" squares last. Press the seam allowances away from the Kitten blocks.

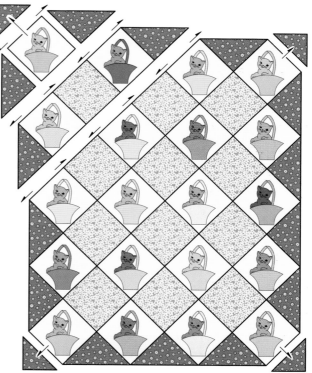

Quilt assembly

4. To trim and straighten the quilt top, align the ¼"
mark on your ruler with the outermost points of
the blocks. Use a rotary cutter to trim any excess
fabric, leaving a ¼"-wide seam allowance. Square
the corners of the quilt top as necessary.

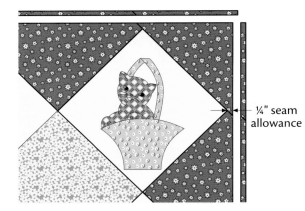

¼" seam
allowance

5. Refer to "Borders" on page 15 to measure, cut, and
sew the 1½"-wide orange strips for the inner border and then the 6½"-wide blue strips for the outer
border. Press all seam allowances toward the newly
added border strips.

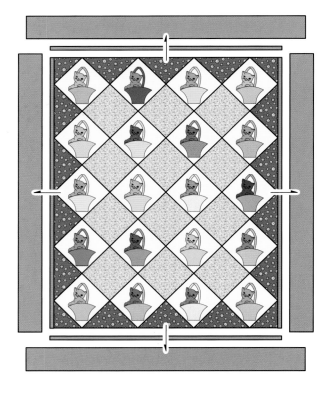

🔲 FINISHING THE QUILT

Referring to "Finishing Techniques" on page 16, cut
and piece the backing fabric and then layer the quilt
top with batting and backing. After basting the layers together, hand or machine quilt as desired; see the
quilting suggestion below. Trim the batting and backing so that the edges are even with the quilt top. Using
the 2"-wide blue strips, sew the binding to the quilt.

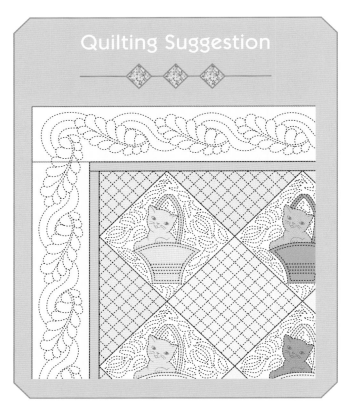

Quilting Suggestion

46

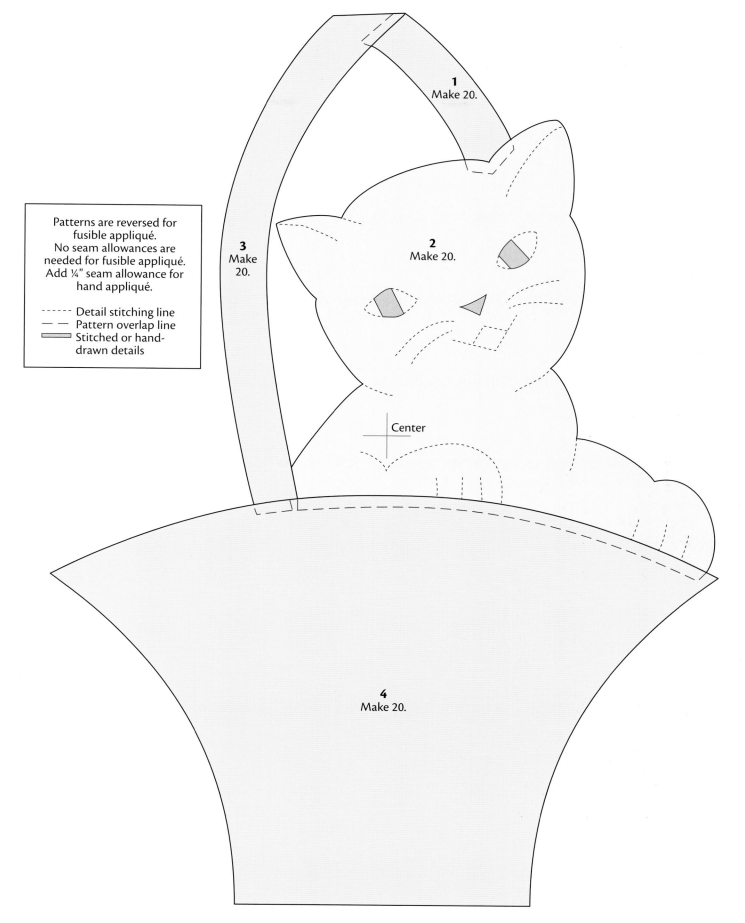

Patterns are reversed for
fusible appliqué.
No seam allowances are
needed for fusible appliqué.
Add ¼" seam allowance for
hand appliqué.

- - - - - Detail stitching line
— — — Pattern overlap line
▭ Stitched or hand-
drawn details

1
Make 20.

2
Make 20.

3
Make
20.

Center

4
Make 20.

BUTTERFLY GARDEN

Made by Nancy Mahoney. Machine quilted by Dawn Kelly.

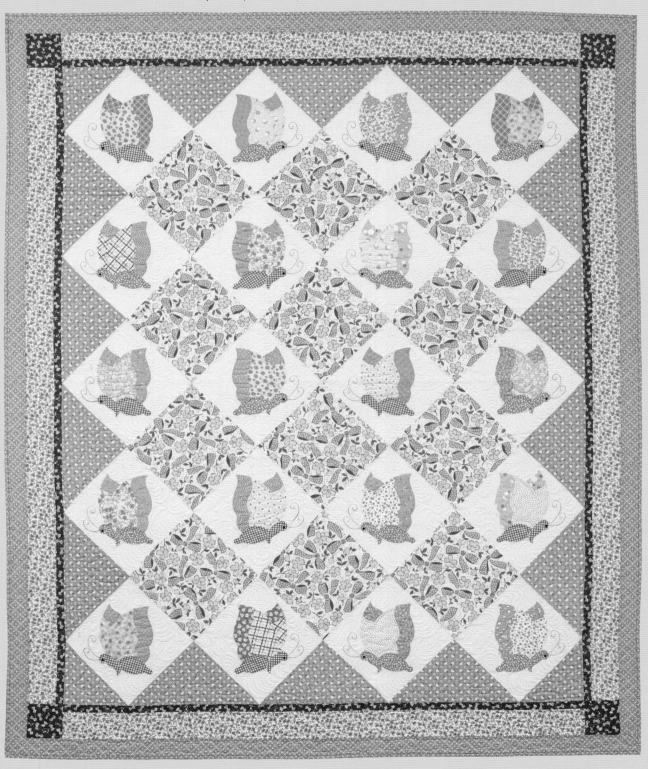

Finished Quilt Size: 65½" x 79" ◆ Finished Block Size: 9½"

You'll be dreaming of butterflies in your garden when you wrap yourself up in this large lap quilt. This charming butterfly design could be obtained from the *Arizona Republic* Household Arts Department for 15 cents and was one of the patterns from Alice Brooks Designs. I selected pink prints from my scrap bag for the sprightly butterflies and then used a fun reproduction feed-sack print for the setting squares. The center design is nicely framed by three narrow borders.

MATERIALS

Yardages are based on 42"-wide fabrics. Fat quarters measure 18" x 21" and fat eighths measure 9" x 21".

2¼ yards of cream solid for block backgrounds

1⅛ yards of medium pink print for outer border and binding

1 yard of pink bows print for setting squares

1 yard of light green print for setting triangles

⅞ yard of green-and-cream floral for middle border

½ yard of dark green print for inner border and corner squares

1 fat quarter *each* of 2 green prints for butterfly appliqués

1 fat eighth *each* of 10 assorted light pink prints and 10 assorted dark pink prints for butterfly appliqués

5¼ yards of fabric for backing

71" x 84" piece of batting

2 yards of 16"-wide fusible web (optional)

Thread in coordinating colors for appliqués

20 black buttons (⅛" diameter) *or* 6-strand black embroidery floss for eyes

Black Pigma pen (size 05) and/or black thread for antenna details

CUTTING

All measurements include ¼"-wide seam allowances. Cut all strips across the width of fabric.

From the cream solid, cut:

◆ 7 strips, 10½" x 42"; crosscut into 20 squares, 10½" x 10½"

From the pink bows print, cut:

◆ 3 strips, 10" x 42"; crosscut into 12 squares, 10" x 10"

From the light green print, cut:

◆ 4 squares, 15" x 15"; cut twice diagonally to yield 16 triangles (You'll have 2 extra triangles.)

◆ 2 squares, 8" x 8"; cut once diagonally to yield 4 triangles

From the dark green print, cut:

◆ 7 strips, 1¼" x 42"

◆ 4 squares, 4⅛" x 4⅛"

From the green-and-cream floral, cut:

◆ 7 strips, 3⅜" x 42"

From the medium pink print, cut:

◆ 8 outer-border strips, 2½" x 42"

◆ 8 binding strips, 2" x 42"

APPLIQUÉING THE BLOCKS

1. Choose your favorite appliqué method and make appliqué templates for the butterfly by tracing the pattern on page 52. Refer to "Appliqué Techniques" on page 7 for details as needed. Make the quantity indicated on the pattern for each shape. Refer to the photo on page 48 for color-placement ideas.

2. Using the pattern as a placement guide, position the butterflies on the 10½" cream squares. Be sure the cream squares are positioned on point. Appliqué the pieces in numerical order as indicated on the pattern.

3. Use the Pigma pen to draw the antennae or, if you prefer, use a straight stitch on your machine or hand embroider a stem stitch. For the eyes, hand embroider a French knot now or add buttons after the quilting is completed.

4. Make 20 Butterfly blocks. Gently press and then trim each block to 10" x 10", referring to "Squaring Up Blocks" on page 7.

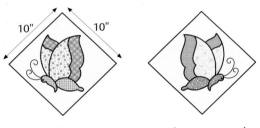

Make 10.   Make 10 reversed.

QUILT-TOP ASSEMBLY

For detailed instructions, refer to "Quilts Set Diagonally" on page 14. The setting triangles have been cut slightly oversize. You will trim them after the quilt center is assembled.

1. Lay out the Butterfly blocks and 10" pink setting squares as shown in the quilt-assembly diagram. Note that the butterflies face each other in the two vertical rows in the quilt center; in the two outer rows, the butterflies face the border. Add the green triangles cut from 15" squares.

2. Sew the blocks, setting squares, and side triangles together into rows. Press the seam allowances away from the Butterfly blocks.

3. Sew the rows together, adding the green triangles cut from 8" squares last. Press the seam allowances away from the Butterfly blocks.

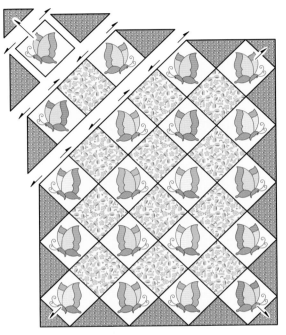

Quilt assembly

4. To trim and straighten the quilt top, align the ¼" mark on your ruler with the outermost points of the blocks. Use a rotary cutter to trim any excess fabric, leaving a ¼"-wide seam allowance. Square the corners of the quilt top as necessary.

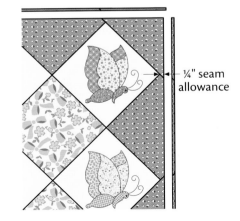

¼" seam allowance

5. Sew two of the 1¼" x 42" dark green strips together end to end. Press the seam allowance open. Sew two 3⅜" x 42" green-and-cream floral strips together end to end; press the seam allowance open. Then sew the long dark green strip to one long side of the green-and-cream floral strip to make a side border strip. Make two side border strips.

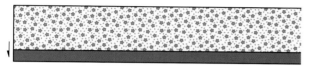

Make 2.

6. Repeat step 5, sewing the remaining three dark green strips end to end; press. Sew the remaining three green-and-cream floral strips together end to end; press. Then sew the long dark green strip and the floral strip together to make one long border strip; press the seam allowance toward the dark green strip.

7. Measure the quilt through the center from side to side. Using the border strip from step 6, cut two strips to that measurement. Sew a 4⅛" dark green square to each end of each border strip. Press the seam allowances toward the border strips. Set these aside for the top and bottom borders.

Make 2.

8. Measure the quilt through the center from top to bottom. Using the side border strips from step 5, cut two strips to that measurement and sew them to the side edges of the quilt top. Press the seam allowances toward the border strips.

9. Sew the top and bottom borders from step 7 to the quilt top; press.

10. Refer to "Borders" on page 15 to measure, cut, and sew the 2½"-wide pink strips for the outer border.

Press all seam allowances toward the newly added border strips.

🌸 FINISHING THE QUILT

Referring to "Finishing Techniques" on page 16, cut and piece the backing fabric and then layer the quilt top with batting and backing. After basting the layers together, hand or machine quilt as desired; see the quilting suggestion below. Trim the batting and backing so that the edges are even with the quilt top. Using the 2"-wide pink strips, sew the binding to the quilt.

Quilting Suggestion

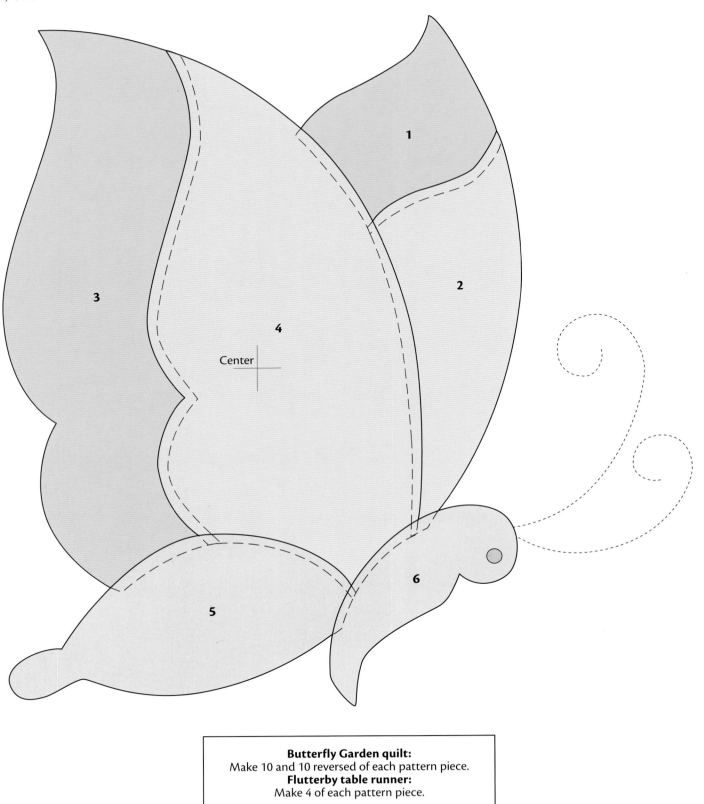

Butterfly Garden quilt:
Make 10 and 10 reversed of each pattern piece.
Flutterby table runner:
Make 4 of each pattern piece.

Patterns are reversed for fusible appliqué.
No seam allowances are needed for fusible appliqué.
Add ¼" seam allowance for hand appliqué.

----- Detail stitching line
— — Pattern overlap line
▬▬▬ Stitched or hand-drawn details

FLUTTERBY TABLE RUNNER

Made by Nancy Mahoney.

Finished Quilt Size: 23½" x 63½"

◆

Finished Block Size: 9½"

This oversize table runner is simply precious and makes a perfect table topper for an afternoon tea with gardening friends. You can also use it as a wall hanging to decorate a narrow space. The prairie points add dimension and are so easy! Plus, with only four blocks to make, it goes together in a snap—a great weekend project.

MATERIALS

Yardages are based on 42"-wide fabrics. Fat quarters measure 18" x 21" and fat eighths measure 9" x 21".

1 yard of dark blue print for prairie points and inner border

1 yard of peach star print for outer border and binding

⅔ yard of cream solid for block backgrounds

¾ yard of light blue print for setting triangles

1 fat quarter *each* of blue print and peach print for butterfly appliqués

1 fat eighth of brown print for butterfly appliqués

1⅞ yards of fabric for backing

29" x 69" piece of batting

½ yard of 16"-wide fusible web (optional)

Thread in coordinating colors for appliqués

4 black buttons (⅛" diameter) or black 6-strand embroidery floss for eyes

Black Pigma pen (size 05) and/or black thread for antenna details

CUTTING

All measurements include ¼"-wide seam allowances. Cut all strips across the width of fabric.

From the cream solid, cut:

◆ 4 squares, 10½" x 10½"

From the light blue print, cut:

◆ 2 squares, 15" x 15"; cut twice diagonally to yield 8 triangles. (You'll have 2 extra triangles.)

◆ 2 squares, 8" x 8"; cut once diagonally to yield 4 triangles

From the dark blue print, cut:

◆ 5 strips, 4½" x 42"; crosscut into 36 squares, 4½" x 4½"

◆ 3 strips, 1¾" x 42"

◆ 1 strip, 1⅝" x 42"

From the peach star print, cut:

◆ 4 strips, 4" x 42"

◆ 5 binding strips, 2" x 42"

APPLIQUÉING THE BLOCKS

1. Choose your favorite appliqué method and make appliqué templates for the butterfly by tracing the pattern on page 52. Refer to "Appliqué Techniques" on page 7 for details as needed. Make the quantity indicated on the pattern for each shape. Refer to the photo on page 53 for color-placement ideas.

2. Using the pattern as a placement guide, position the butterflies on the 10½" cream squares. Be sure the cream squares are positioned on point. Appliqué the pieces in numerical order as indicated on the pattern.

3. Use the Pigma pen to draw the antennae, and then sew a straight stitch on your machine or hand embroider a stem stitch over the line. For the eyes, hand embroider a French knot now or add a button after the quilting is completed.

4. Make four Butterfly blocks. Gently press and then trim each block to 10" x 10", referring to "Squaring Up Blocks" on page 7.

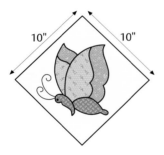

Make 4.

QUILT-TOP ASSEMBLY

The setting triangles have been cut slightly oversize. You will trim them after the quilt center is assembled.

1. Assemble and sew the appliqué blocks and six of the light blue triangles cut from 15" squares into a vertical row as shown; press.

2. Sew the light blue triangles cut from 8" squares to the corners as shown; press. Make one vertical row.

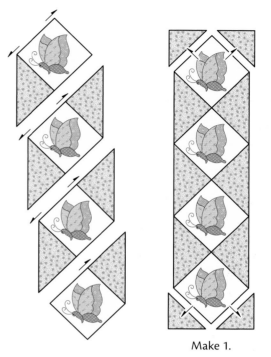

Make 1.

3. Square up the row by trimming the excess triangle fabrics, leaving a ¼" seam allowance all the way around the pieced strip.

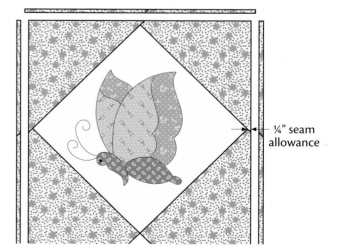

¼" seam allowance

4. Sew the three 1¾" x 42" dark blue strips together end to end to make one continuous strip. Measure the length of the block row through the center and cut two strips from the long strip to that measurement. Sew the strips to the side edges of the block row. Press the seam allowances toward the border strips.

5. Measure the block row from side to side, including the borders you just added. Using the 1⅝" x 42" dark blue strip, cut two strips to that measurement. Sew the strips to the top and bottom edges. Press the seam allowances toward the border strips. The quilt top should measure 16½" x 56½".

6. To make the prairie points, fold each 4½" dark blue square in half horizontally, wrong sides together; press. Then fold the two ends in toward the center on the diagonal as shown; press. Make 36 prairie points.

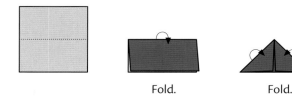

Fold.   Fold.

7. Starting at one corner of the quilt, pin the cut edge of each prairie point, folded side up, to the cut edge of the quilt top. Position the prairie points evenly along each side. (They will overlap about ¼".) Using a walking foot and a scant ¼"-wide seam allowance, stitch the prairie points to all four edges of the quilt.

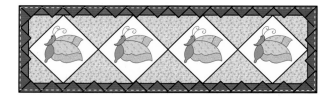

8. Refer to "Borders" on page 15 to measure, cut, and sew the 4"-wide peach strips for the outer border. Press all seam allowances toward the dark blue border strips.

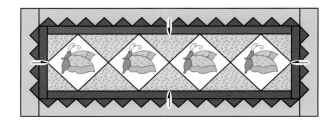

FINISHING THE QUILT

Referring to "Finishing Techniques" on page 16, cut and piece the backing fabric, and then layer the quilt top with batting and backing. After basting the layers together, hand or machine quilt as desired; see the quilting suggestion below. Trim the batting and backing so that the edges are even with the quilt top. Using the 2"-wide peach strips, sew the binding to the quilt.

Quilting Suggestion

RIDE 'EM COWBOY

Made by Nancy Mahoney. Machine quilted by Dawn Kelly.

Finished Quilt Size: 64¼" x 77¾" ◆ Finished Block Size: 9½"

The *Arizona Republic* described this Alice Brooks design as follows: "Any young 'cowboy' will approve of this appliqué quilt for there's plenty of action! Use bright scraps for the cowboy patches—plain material for horses." I enhanced the cowboy action by "tilting" the appliqué blocks and setting them with blue-and-red Hourglass blocks and pieced side triangles. The cowboys are made from bright scraps of blue and red prints, with one brown print used for all the horses. I repeated the blue dot fabric in the outer border to make this fun and whimsical quilt a favorite for your little cowboy—or cowgirl!

◼ MATERIALS

Yardages are based on 42"-wide fabrics.

3⅞ yards of blue dot print for blocks, outer border, and binding

1½ yards of cream solid for block backgrounds

1¼ yards of red-and-cream print for Hourglass blocks and setting triangles

1¼ yards of light blue print for Hourglass blocks and setting triangles

1 yard of brown print for horse appliqués

1 rectangle, 5" x 6", *each* of 10 assorted red prints and 10 assorted blue prints for cowboy appliqués

Scrap of black solid for cowboy boot appliqués

5¼ yards of fabric for backing*

69" x 83" piece of batting

2 yards of 16"-wide fusible web (optional)

Thread in coordinating colors for appliqués

Black and brown Pigma pens (size 05) and/or 6-strand embroidery floss for appliqué details

If your fabric is at least 42" wide, 4½ yards will be enough.

◼ CUTTING

All measurements include ¼"-wide seam allowances. Cut all strips across the width of fabric unless otherwise indicated.

From the cream solid, cut:

◆ 5 strips, 9½" x 42"; crosscut into 20 squares, 9½" x 9½"

From the *lengthwise* grain of the blue dot print, cut:

◆ 4 strips, 5½" x 70"

◆ 5 binding strips, 2" x 60"

From the *crosswise* grain of the remaining blue dot print, cut:

◆ 24 strips, 2¼" x 42"; crosscut into:

• 40 rectangles, 2¼" x 12⅛"

• 40 rectangles, 2¼" x 8⅝"

From the red-and-cream print, cut:

◆ 6 squares, 11" x 11"

◆ 8 squares, 7¾" x 7¾"; cut once diagonally to yield 16 triangles

From the light blue print, cut:

◆ 6 squares, 11" x 11"

◆ 8 squares, 7¾" x 7¾"; cut once diagonally to yield 16 triangles

APPLIQUÉING THE BLOCKS

1. Choose your favorite appliqué method and make appliqué templates for the cowboy, boots, and horse by tracing the pattern on page 62. Refer to "Appliqué Techniques" on page 7 for details as needed. Make the quantity indicated on the pattern for each shape. Refer to the photo on page 57 for color-placement ideas.

2. Using the pattern as a placement guide, position the horses, cowboys, and boots on the 9½" cream squares. Be sure the cream squares are positioned on point. Appliqué the pieces in numerical order as indicated on the pattern.

3. Use the black Pigma pen to draw the horse and cowboy details or, if you prefer, sew a straight stitch on your machine or hand embroider a stem stitch over the lines. Use the brown Pigma pen to draw the hill.

4. Make 20 appliqué blocks. Gently press and then trim each block to 8⅝" x 8⅝", referring to "Squaring Up Blocks" on page 7.

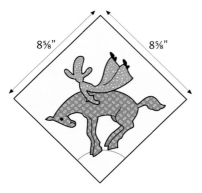

Make 20.

COMPLETING THE BLOCKS

1. Sew a 2¼" x 8⅝" blue dot rectangle to opposite sides of an appliqué block. Press the seam allowances toward the rectangles. Sew a 2¼" x 12⅛" blue dot rectangle to the top and bottom edges; press.

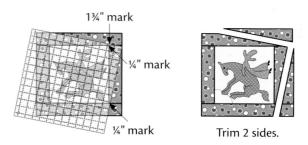

2. Position a 12½" square ruler on top of the block from step 1 at a pleasing angle so that the ¼" marks on the ruler are aligned with the corners of the cream square as shown. I aligned the 1¾" mark of the ruler over the upper corner. Trim two sides of the block.

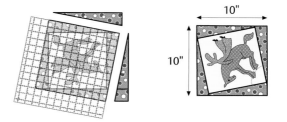

Trim 2 sides.

3. Turn the block, realign the ruler, and trim the two remaining sides. The block should measure 10" square.

4. Repeat steps 1–3 for the other 19 Cowboy blocks.

◆ MAKING THE HOURGLASS BLOCKS

1. Draw a diagonal line from corner to corner on the wrong side of each 11" light blue square. Place each marked square right sides together with an 11" red-and-cream square. Stitch ¼" from both sides of the line. Cut the squares apart on the marked line, and press the seam allowances toward the red-and-cream triangles.

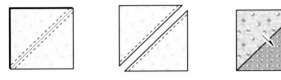

Make 12.

2. Cut the half-square-triangle units from step 1 in half diagonally as shown.

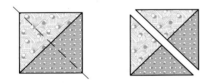

3. Sew the triangle units together as shown and press. Trim the blocks to 10" square. Make 12 Hourglass blocks.

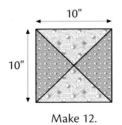

Make 12.

◆ QUILT-TOP ASSEMBLY

For detailed instructions, refer to "Quilts Set Diagonally" on page 14. The setting triangles have been cut slightly oversize. You will trim them after the quilt center is assembled.

1. To make the side triangle units, sew one 7¾" light blue triangle and one 7¾" red-and-cream triangle together along one short side. Set aside two light blue triangles and two red-and-cream triangles to use as the corner triangles. Make the number of triangle units indicated. Press the seam allowances toward the red.

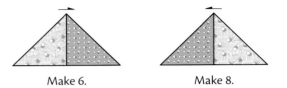

Make 6.   Make 8.

2. Refer to the quilt assembly diagram to arrange the Cowboy blocks, the Hourglass blocks, and the side triangle units from step 1 into diagonal rows as shown.

3. Stitch the blocks and side triangles together into rows. Press the seam allowances away from the Cowboy blocks.

4. Stitch the rows together, adding the corner triangles last. Press toward the corners.

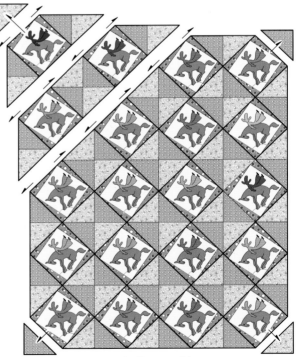

Quilt assembly

60

5. To trim and straighten the quilt top, align the ¼" mark on your ruler with the outermost points of the blocks. Use a rotary cutter to trim any excess fabric, leaving a ¼"-wide seam allowance. Square the corners of the quilt top as necessary.

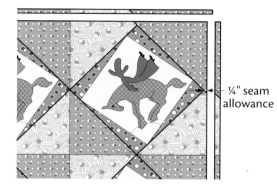

¼" seam allowance

6. Refer to "Borders" on page 15 to measure, cut, and sew the 5½"-wide blue strips for the outer border. Press all seam allowances toward the blue border strips.

FINISHING THE QUILT

Referring to "Finishing Techniques" on page 16, cut and piece the backing fabric and then layer the quilt top with batting and backing. After basting the layers together, hand or machine quilt as desired; see the quilting suggestion below. Trim the batting and backing so that the edges are even with the quilt top. Using the 2"-wide blue dot strips, sew the binding to the quilt.

Quilting Suggestion

61

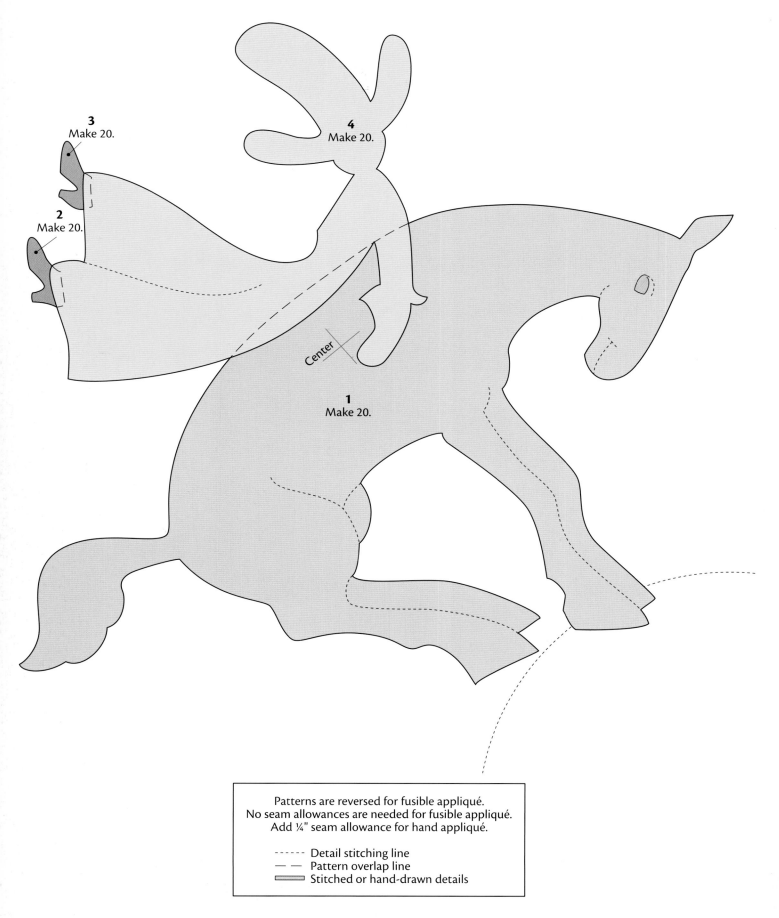

3
Make 20.

4
Make 20.

2
Make 20.

Center

1
Make 20.

Patterns are reversed for fusible appliqué.
No seam allowances are needed for fusible appliqué.
Add ¼" seam allowance for hand appliqué.

- - - - Detail stitching line
— — Pattern overlap line
▭ Stitched or hand-drawn details

PEONY GARDEN

Made by Nancy Mahoney. Machine quilted by Dawn Kelly.

Finished Quilt Size: 72⅝" x 84⅝" ◆ Finished Block Size: 8½"

This delicate Alice Brooks pattern was described in the *Arizona Republic* as "Garden Favorite—and it will be your favorite quilt too—gives you peonies in patchwork. Do the flowers and the leaves in two shades of color." The pattern was originally a pieced block, with complex construction, curved seams, and odd angles. That was yesterday—this is today. If our grandmothers had had our modern tools and supplies, I'm sure they would have put them to use when making these blocks. I used fusible web to appliqué the Peony blocks and then combined them with Criss Cross blocks to create this wonderful quilt. Easy pieced setting triangles give the illusion of a scalloped border, adding to the traditional magic.

☙ MATERIALS

Yardages are based on 42"-wide fabrics. Fat eighths measure 9" x 21".

4 yards of cream solid for appliqué block backgrounds, Criss Cross blocks, and setting triangles

3 yards of purple-and-cream dot print for setting triangles, outer border, and binding

⅞ yard of small-scale purple dot print for Criss Cross blocks and setting triangles

1 fat eighth *each* of 5 dark green prints and 5 light green prints for leaf appliqués

1 rectangle, 6" x 8", *each* of 12 assorted dark purple prints, 12 assorted dark pink prints, 3 orange prints, and 3 dark yellow prints for flower appliqués

1 rectangle, 4" x 6", *each* of 12 assorted light purple prints, 12 assorted light pink prints, 3 peach prints, and 3 light yellow prints for flower appliqués

5½ yards of fabric for backing

78" x 90" piece of batting

5 yards of 16"-wide fusible web (optional)

Thread in coordinating colors for appliqués

☙ CUTTING

All measurements include ¼"-wide seam allowances. Cut all strips across the width of fabric unless otherwise indicated.

From the cream solid, cut:

◆ 8 strips, 9½" x 42"; crosscut into 30 squares, 9½" x 9½"

◆ 4 strips, 6" x 42"; crosscut *2 strips* into 40 rectangles, 2" x 6"

◆ 2 strips, 3" x 42"

◆ 14 strips, 2" x 42"; crosscut *10 strips* into:
  • 4 rectangles, 2" x 9½"
  • 36 rectangles, 2" x 8½"

From the small-scale purple dot print, cut:

◆ 2 strips, 3" x 42"

◆ 9 strips, 2" x 42"; crosscut *1 strip* into 18 squares, 2" x 2"

From the *lengthwise* grain of the purple-and-cream dot print, cut:

◆ 4 strips, 6½" x 78"

◆ 5 squares, 11¼" x 11¼"; cut twice diagonally to yield 20 triangles (You'll have 2 extra triangles.)

◆ 2 squares, 6½" x 6½"; cut once diagonally to yield 4 triangles

From the *crosswise* grain of the remaining purple-and-cream dot print, cut:

◆ 9 strips, 2" x 42"

APPLIQUÉING THE BLOCKS

1. Choose your favorite appliqué method and make appliqué templates for the flower and leaves by tracing the pattern on page 68. Refer to "Appliqué Techniques" on page 7 for details as needed. Make the quantity indicated on the pattern for each shape. Refer to the photo on page 63 for color-placement ideas.

2. Using the pattern as a placement guide, position the flowers and leaves on the 9½" cream squares. Be sure the cream squares are positioned on point. Appliqué the pieces in numerical order as indicated on the pattern.

3. Make 30 Peony blocks. Gently press and then trim each block to 9" x 9", referring to "Squaring Up Blocks" on page 7.

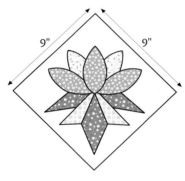

Make 30.

MAKING THE CRISS CROSS BLOCKS

1. Sew a 2" x 42" cream strip to both long sides of a 3" x 42" small-scale dot strip as shown to make strip set A; press. Make two. Crosscut the strip sets into 20 segments, 3" wide.

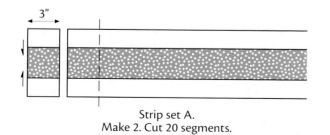

Strip set A.
Make 2. Cut 20 segments.

2. Sew a 2" x 42" small-scale dot strip to both long sides of a 3" x 42" cream strip as shown to make strip set B; press. Make two. Crosscut the strip sets into 40 segments, 2" wide.

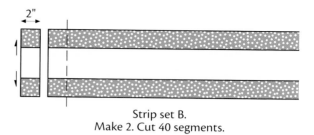

Strip set B.
Make 2. Cut 40 segments.

3. Arrange one strip set A segment and two strip set B segments as shown. Sew the segments together to make a nine-patch unit; press. Make 20.

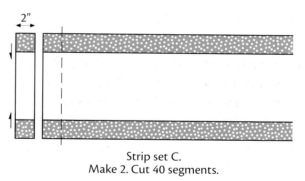

Make 20.

4. Sew a 2" x 42" small-scale dot strip to both long sides of a 6" x 42" cream strip as shown to make strip set C; press. Make two. Crosscut the strip sets into 40 segments, 2" wide.

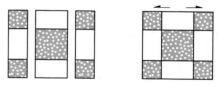

Strip set C.
Make 2. Cut 40 segments.

5. Arrange and sew one nine-patch unit from step 3, two strip set C segments, and two 2" x 6" cream rectangles together as shown; press. Make 20 Criss Cross blocks. The blocks should measure 9" x 9".

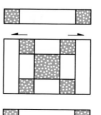 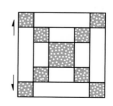

Make 20.

MAKING THE SETTING TRIANGLES

1. Arrange and sew one 2" small-scale dot square, two 2" x 8½" cream rectangles, and one 11¼" purple-and-cream triangle as shown; press. Make 18 side triangles.

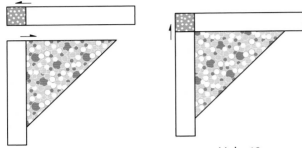

Make 18.

2. Fold each 2" x 9½" cream rectangle in half and lightly crease to mark the center. Fold each 6½" purple-and-cream triangle in half and lightly crease to mark the center of the long side. Sew a rectangle to each triangle as shown, matching the center creases; press. Make four corner triangles.

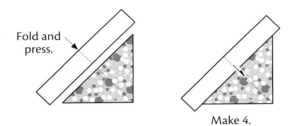

Fold and press.

Make 4.

QUILT-TOP ASSEMBLY

For detailed instructions, refer to "Quilts Set Diagonally" on page 14.

1. Refer to the quilt assembly diagram to arrange the Peony blocks, Criss Cross blocks, and pieced side triangles in diagonal rows as shown.

2. Sew the pieces in each row together, pressing the seam allowances toward the Peony blocks. Sew the rows together and press the seam allowances in one direction. Add the corner triangles last; press. Note that the edges of the quilt top will be uneven at this point.

Quilt assembly

3. To trim and straighten the quilt top, align the ¼" mark on your ruler with the outermost points of the Peony blocks. Use a rotary cutter to trim any excess fabric, leaving a ¼"-wide seam allowance. Square the corners of the quilt top as necessary.

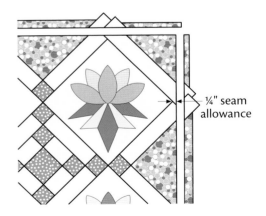

¼" seam allowance

4. Refer to "Borders" on page 15 to measure, cut, and sew the 6½"-wide purple-and-cream strips for the outer border. Press all seam allowances toward the outer-border strips.

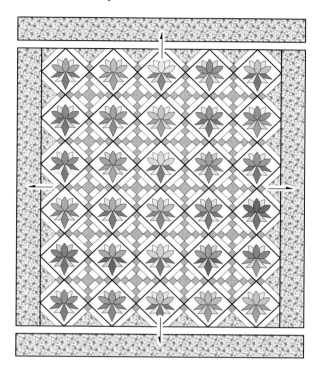

FINISHING THE QUILT

Referring to "Finishing Techniques" on page 16, cut and piece the backing fabric, and then layer the quilt top with batting and backing. After basting the layers together, hand or machine quilt as desired; see the quilting suggestion below. Trim the batting and backing so that the edges are even with the quilt top. Using the 2"-wide purple-and-cream strips, sew the binding to the quilt.

Quilting Suggestion

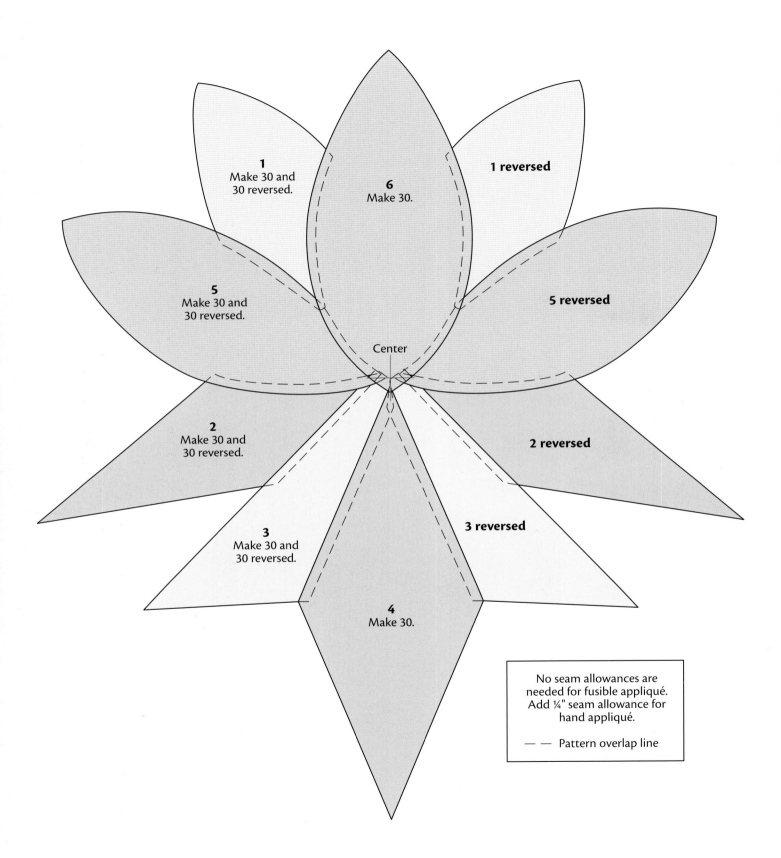

1
Make 30 and
30 reversed.

1 reversed

6
Make 30.

5
Make 30 and
30 reversed.

5 reversed

Center

2
Make 30 and
30 reversed.

2 reversed

3
Make 30 and
30 reversed.

3 reversed

4
Make 30.

No seam allowances are
needed for fusible appliqué.
Add ¼" seam allowance for
hand appliqué.

— — — Pattern overlap line

COLONIAL SCRAP BASKETS

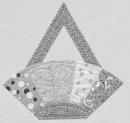

Made by Nancy Mahoney. Machine quilted by Karen Housel.

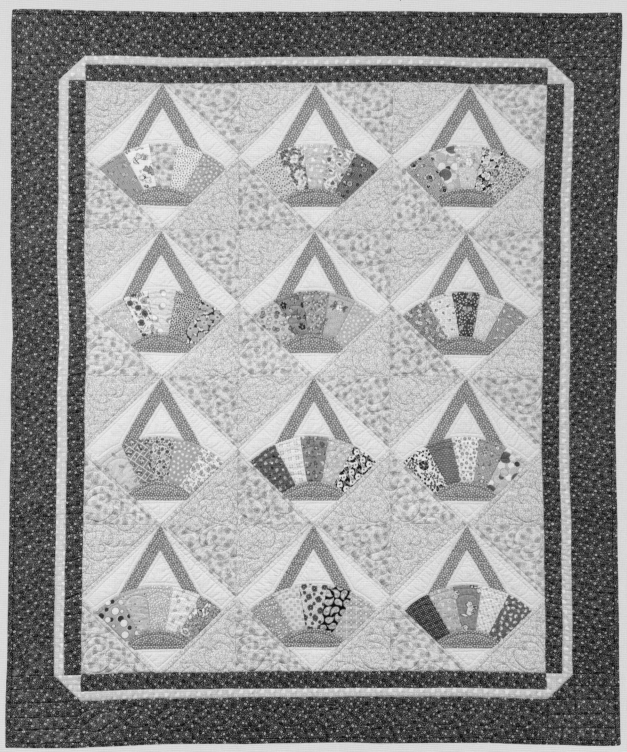

Finished Quilt Size: 45½" x 56¾" ◆ Finished Block Size: 8"

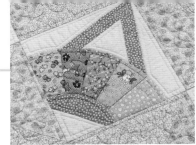

To describe this Alice Brooks pattern, the *Arizona Republic* wrote, "Show your skill as an American needlewoman—use up scraps of material to make a lovely quilt. It will be an easy task if you select this scrap quilt, Colonial Basket." For this striking Basket block, I decided on purple, green, and aqua scraps with a few scraps of peach and orange for a little variety. The yellow background makes the Basket blocks stand out from the Hourglass blocks and pieced triangles. An easy pieced border was just the ticket for this marvelous quilt.

MATERIALS

Yardages are based on 42"-wide fabrics.

1½ yards of dark purple print for borders and binding

⅞ yard of yellow solid for block backgrounds

⅝ yard of light green print for Hourglass blocks and setting triangles

⅝ yard of light purple print for Hourglass blocks and setting triangles

⅜ yard of purple dot print for basket appliqués (handles and bases)

⅓ yard of yellow print for middle border

1 rectangle, 3½" x 5", *each* of 60 assorted purple, green, aqua, and peach prints for basket appliqués

3¼ yards of fabric for backing

51" x 62" piece of batting

1⅞ yards of 16"-wide fusible web (optional)

Thread in coordinating colors for appliqués

CUTTING

All measurements include ¼"-wide seam allowances. Cut all strips across the width of fabric unless otherwise indicated.

From the yellow solid, cut:

◆ 3 strips, 9" x 42"; crosscut into 12 squares, 9" x 9"

From the light green print, cut:

◆ 3 squares, 9½" x 9½"

◆ 6 squares, 6⅝" x 6⅝"; cut once diagonally to yield 12 triangles

From the light purple print, cut:

◆ 3 squares, 9½" x 9½"

◆ 6 squares, 6⅝" x 6⅝"; cut once diagonally to yield 12 triangles

From the *lengthwise* grain of dark purple print, cut:

◆ 2 outer-border strips, 4" x 50"

◆ 2 outer-border strips, 4" x 40"

◆ 5 binding strips, 2" x 50"

◆ 2 inner-border strips, 1¾" x 50"

◆ 2 inner-border strips, 1¾" x 40"

◆ 4 squares, 6" x 6"

From the yellow print, cut:

◆ 5 strips, 1¼" x 42"

◆ 4 squares, 2½" x 2½"

◼ PAPER PIECING THE BASKETS

1. Make 12 copies of the basket foundation pattern on page 74.

2. Turn the foundation so that the blank (unmarked) side of the paper faces up. Position one of the 3½" x 5" rectangles for piece 1, right side up, to cover area 1. Using the light from your sewing machine or another light source, look through the fabric and paper to make sure that area 1 is completely covered, plus an ample seam allowance. Turn the paper and fabric over, being careful not to move the fabric, and pin the fabric in place through the marked side of the paper.

3. Once again, turn the foundation over to the unmarked side. Look through the paper and place a fabric rectangle for piece 2, right side up, over area 2. When the fabric for piece 2 is properly positioned, flip it on top of piece 1, right sides together.

4. Hold the layers in place, turn the foundation over, and carefully position the unit under your sewing machine's presser foot, paper side up. Sew on the line between areas 1 and 2, starting ¼" before the line and extending ¼" beyond.

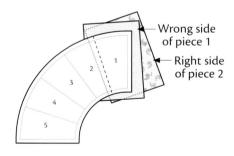

Wrong side of piece 1

Right side of piece 2

5. Open piece 2 and remove the pin from piece 1. Hold the block up to the light source and look through the fabric to be sure the edges of piece 2 extend beyond the seam lines for area 2 on the foundation. Refold the fabrics with right sides together and then fold the paper back to reveal the seam allowance. Place a ruler along the edge of the paper and trim the seam allowance to ¼".

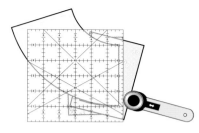

6. Open piece 2 and press the seam allowance to one side with a dry iron. Trim any excess fabric if necessary.

7. Repeat steps 3–6 to add pieces 3, 4, and 5. Remove the foundation paper. Make 12 scrappy basket units.

Make 12.

◼ APPLIQUÉING THE BLOCKS

1. Choose your favorite appliqué method and make appliqué templates for the handle and base of the basket by tracing the pattern on page 75. Refer to "Appliqué Techniques" on page 7 for details as needed. Using the purple dot fabric, make the quantity indicated on the pattern for each shape.

2. Using the pattern as a placement guide, position the handles on the 9" yellow squares and appliqué in place. Be sure the yellow squares are positioned on point.

3. Fold the seam allowance along the curved top edge of the basket unit to the wrong side and press in place to make a finished edge. It doesn't matter if the seam allowance is not a uniform width. If you are using fusible web for the foundation-pieced unit, re-press the seam allowances of the basket unit open; apply fusible web to the wrong side and trim the seam allowance off the top curved edge only.

4. Position the baskets on the yellow squares, using a placement guide as needed, and appliqué in place along the top curved edge. Position the basket bases and appliqué in place along the top curved edge and the bottom. Note that the sides of the basket and the basket base will be sewn into the block seam.

5. Make 12 Colonial Basket blocks. Gently press and then trim each block to 8½" x 8½", referring to "Squaring Up Blocks" on page 7.

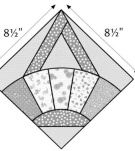

8½"   8½"

Make 12.

MAKING THE HOURGLASS BLOCKS

1. Draw a diagonal line from corner to corner on the wrong side of each 9½" light green square. Place each marked square right sides together with a 9½" light purple square. Stitch ¼" from both sides of the line. Cut the squares apart on the marked line and press the seam allowance toward the light purple triangle.

Make 6.

2. Cut the half-square-triangle units from step 1 in half diagonally as shown.

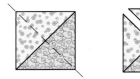

3. Sew the triangle units together as shown and press. Trim the block to 8½" square. Make six Hourglass blocks.

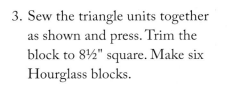

8½"

8½"

Make 6.

QUILT-TOP ASSEMBLY

For detailed instructions, refer to "Quilts Set Diagonally" on page 14.

1. To make the side triangle units, sew one 6⅝" light green triangle and one 6⅝" light purple triangle together along one short side. Set aside two light green triangles and two light purple triangles to use as the corner triangles. Make the number of triangle units indicated. Press the seam allowances toward the purple.

Make 6.   Make 4.

2. Refer to the quilt assembly diagram to arrange the Colonial Basket blocks, the Hourglass blocks, and the side triangle units from step 1 in diagonal rows as shown.

3. Stitch the blocks and side triangles together into rows. Press the seam allowances toward the Colonial Basket blocks.

4. Stitch the rows together, adding the corner triangles last. Press the seam allowances toward the corners.

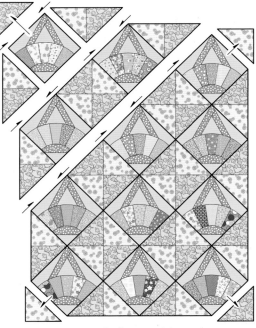

Quilt assembly

72

5. Sew the 1¼" x 42" yellow strips together end to end, pressing the seam allowances open. From this long strip, cut two strips, approximately 50" long, and two strips, approximately 40" long.

6. Sew a 50"-long yellow strip to one long side of a 1¾" x 50" dark purple strip; press. Then sew a 4" x 50" dark purple strip to the other long side of the yellow strip as shown to make a long border strip; press. Make two long border strips.

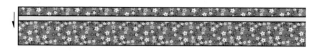

7. Repeat step 6 using the 40"-long yellow strips, the 1¾" x 40" dark purple strips, and the 4" x 40" dark purple strips. Make two short border strips.

8. To make the corner blocks, draw a diagonal line from corner to corner on the wrong side of each 2½" yellow square. Place a marked square on one corner of each 6" dark purple square as shown, right sides together. Sew along the drawn line. Trim away the excess fabric, leaving a ¼" seam allowance. Press the seam allowance toward the yellow.

Make 4.

9. Measure the quilt through the center from side to side. Trim the short border strips from step 7 to that measurement. Sew a corner square from step 8 to the ends of each border strip as shown. Press the seam allowances toward the border strip. Set these aside for the top and bottom borders.

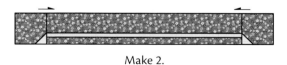

Make 2.

10. Measure the quilt through the center from top to bottom. Trim the long border strips from step 6 to that measurement and sew them to side edges of quilt top. Press the seam allowances toward the border strips.

11. Sew the top and bottom borders from step 9 to the quilt top; press the seam allowances toward the border strips.

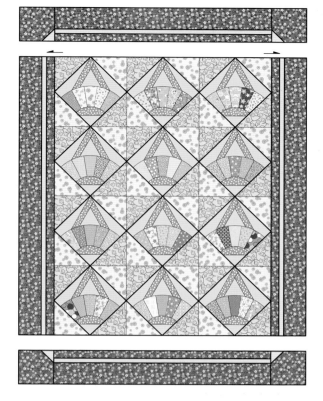

◼ FINISHING THE QUILT

Referring to "Finishing Techniques" on page 16, cut and piece the backing fabric and then layer the quilt top with batting and backing. After basting the layers together, hand or machine quilt as desired; see the quilting suggestion below. Trim the batting and backing so that the edges are even with the quilt top. Using the 2"-wide dark purple strips, sew the binding to the quilt.

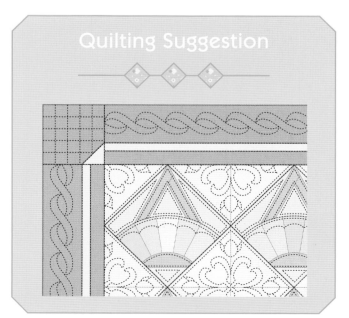

Quilting Suggestion

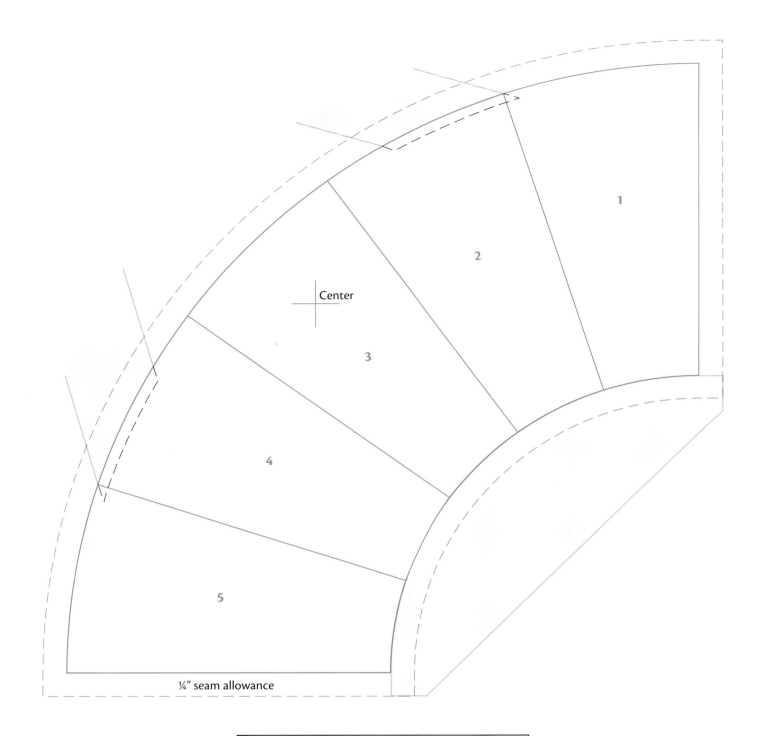

¼" seam allowance

Paper-piecing pattern

Colonial Scrap Basket: Make 12 of each.
Fandango: Make 16 of each.

— — Pattern overlap line
Paper-piecing sewing line
— — Paper-piecing cutting line

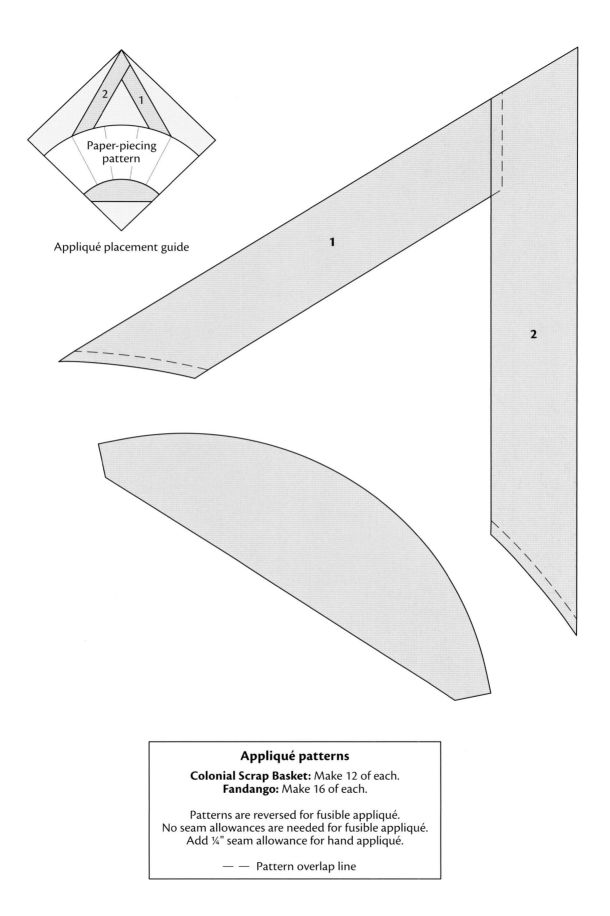

Paper-piecing pattern

Appliqué placement guide

1

2

Appliqué patterns

Colonial Scrap Basket: Make 12 of each.
Fandango: Make 16 of each.

Patterns are reversed for fusible appliqué.
No seam allowances are needed for fusible appliqué.
Add ¼" seam allowance for hand appliqué.

— — Pattern overlap line

FANDANGO

Made by Nancy Mahoney. Machine quilted by Nanette Moore.

Finished Quilt Size: 48" x 48" ◆ Finished Block Size: 8"

The basket design from "Colonial Scrap Baskets" on page 69 does double duty by providing the blocks for this fabulous wall hanging. For this quilt, I used scraps of blue, red, and pink prints, plus a few yellow prints to add a little zip, and a cream for the block background. Then I set the blocks with a narrow cream sashing and—WOW! I love how the baskets form a circle. Rummaging through my scrap bag, I found some leftover strip sets from another quilt, and I knew they'd be perfect for a checked border. A soft, light blue print in the outer border was all it took to complete the enchantment.

▨ MATERIALS

Yardages are based on 42"-wide fabrics. Fat eighths measure 9" x 21".

2 yards of cream solid for block backgrounds, sashing, and borders

1⅓ yards of light blue print for outer border

⅝ yard of dark blue print for corner squares and binding

½ yard of medium blue print for basket appliqués (handles and bases)

1 fat eighth *each* of 12 assorted blue prints for basket appliqués and checked border

1 rectangle, 3½" x 5", *each* of 68 assorted blue, pink, red, and yellow prints for basket appliqués

3⅜ yards of fabric for backing

53" x 53" piece of batting

2½ yards of 16"-wide fusible web (optional)

Thread in coordinating colors for appliqués

▨ CUTTING

All measurements include ¼"-wide seam allowances. Cut all strips across the width of fabric unless otherwise indicated.

From the cream solid, cut:

◆ 4 strips, 9" x 42"; crosscut into 16 squares, 9" x 9"

◆ 4 strips, 2" x 42"; crosscut into 12 pieces, 2" x 13"

◆ 9 strips, 1⅜" x 42"

◆ 6 strips, 1¼" x 42"; crosscut *3 strips* into 12 pieces, 1¼" x 8½"

From *each* of the assorted blue print fat eighths, cut:

◆ 1 strip, 2" x 13" (12 total)

◆ 1 rectangle, 3½" x 5" (12 total)

From the *lengthwise* grain of the light blue print, cut:

◆ 4 strips, 3⅞" x 45"

From the dark blue print, cut:

◆ 6 binding strips, 2" x 42"

◆ 4 squares, 3⅞" x 3⅞"

◼ PAPER PIECING THE BASKETS

1. Make 16 copies of the basket foundation pattern on page 74.

2. Refer to the section "Paper Piecing the Baskets" on page 71 of "Colonial Scrap Baskets." Following the instructions and illustrations, make 16 scrappy basket units.

◼ APPLIQUÉING THE BLOCKS

1. Choose your favorite appliqué method and make appliqué templates for the handle and base of the basket by tracing the pattern on page 75. Refer to "Appliqué Techniques" on page 7 for details as needed. Make the quantity indicated on the pattern for each shape.

2. Using the pattern as a placement guide, position the handles on the 9" cream square and appliqué in place. Be sure the cream square is positioned on point.

3. Fold the seam allowance along the curved top edge of the basket unit to the wrong side and press in place to make a finished edge. It doesn't matter if the seam allowance is not a uniform width. If you are using fusible web for the foundation-pieced unit, re-press the seam allowances of the basket unit open; apply fusible web to the wrong side and trim the seam allowance off the top curved edge only.

4. Position the basket on the cream square, using a placement guide as needed, and appliqué in place along the top curved edge. Position the basket base and appliqué in place along the top curved edge and the bottom. Note that the sides of the basket and basket base will be sewn into the block seam.

5. Make 16 Colonial Basket blocks. Gently press and then trim each block to 8½" x 8½", referring to "Squaring Up Blocks" on page 7.

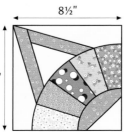

Make 16.

◼ QUILT-TOP ASSEMBLY

For detailed instructions, refer to "Quilts with Sashing Strips" on page 14.

1. Arrange and sew three 1¼" x 8½" cream sashing strips and four blocks, alternating them and rotating the blocks 90° as shown to make a block row; press. Make four rows.

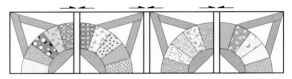

Make 4.

2. Measure the length of each of the four block rows. If they differ, calculate the average and consider this the length. Cut the three 1¼" x 42" cream strips to the length of your row measurement.

3. Sew the block rows and the three sashing strips from step 2 together, alternating them as shown in the quilt assembly diagram. Press the seam allowances toward the sashing strips.

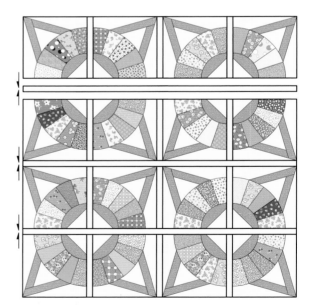

Quilt assembly

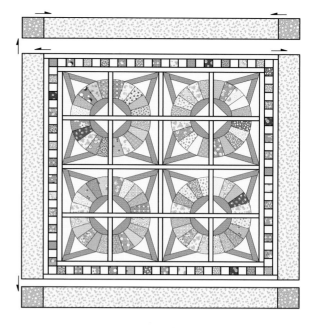

ADDING THE BORDERS

1. Refer to "Borders" on page 15 to measure, cut, and sew four of the 1⅜"-wide cream strips for the inner border. Press all seam allowances toward the border strips. The quilt top should measure 36½" x 36½", which includes seam allowances.

2. Sew a 2" x 13" blue strip to one long side of each 2" x 13" cream strip to make 12 strip sets. Press the seam allowances toward the blue strips. Crosscut the strip sets into 50 segments, 2" wide.

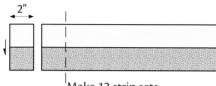

Make 12 strip sets.
Cut 50 segments.

3. Randomly sew 12 segments from step 2 together end to end to make a side border strip. Press the seam allowances in one direction. Make two border strips and sew them to the side edges of the quilt top.

4. Randomly sew 13 segments from step 2 together end to end to make a border strip; press. Make two border strips and sew them to the top and bottom of the quilt top. Refer to the photo on page 76 for color positioning as needed.

5. Measure, cut, and sew the remaining five 1⅜"-wide cream strips to the quilt top. Press all seam allowances toward the border strips you just added.

6. Measure the quilt through the center from side to side and from top to bottom. If the measurements differ, calculate the average and consider this the length. Trim the 3⅞" x 45" light blue strips to that measurement. Sew an outer-border strip to the side edges of the quilt top. Sew a 3⅞" dark blue square to the ends of each remaining border strip, and then sew them to the top and bottom of the quilt top. Press all seam allowances toward the outer-border strips.

FINISHING THE QUILT

Referring to "Finishing Techniques" on page 16, cut and piece the backing fabric and then layer the quilt top with batting and backing. After basting the layers together, hand or machine quilt as desired; see the quilting suggestion below. Trim the batting and backing so that the edges are even with the quilt top. Using the 2"-wide dark blue strips, sew the binding to the quilt.

Quilting Suggestion

TULIP PATCH

Designed by Nancy Mahoney, made by Loretta Sylvester, and machine quilted by Kelly Wise.

Finished Quilt Size: 78¾" x 91⅜" ◆ Finished Block Size: 9"

This captivating Tulip block was printed without a byline; however, the distinctive style is similar to other blocks published under the Alice Brooks name. During the 1930s, realistic-looking tulips were a favorite appliqué design. For this quilt, I nestled the graceful tulips amid scrappy Nine Patch blocks. Loretta selected a variety of green prints for the leaves, with a red plaid and a pink print for all the flowers. Then she selected a wide variety of scraps for the Nine Patch blocks. The aqua inner border and wide yellow outer border frame the blocks to give this bright, perky quilt the perfect finishing touch.

❖ MATERIALS

Yardages are based on 42"-wide fabrics. Fat quarters measure 18" x 21" and fat eighths measure 9" x 21".

4 yards of cream solid for Tulip blocks, Nine Patch blocks, and setting triangles

2½ yards of yellow floral for outer border

⅝ yard of aqua floral for inner border

1 fat quarter of red plaid for tulip appliqués

1 fat quarter of pink print for tulip appliqués

1 fat eighth *each* of 20 assorted green prints for leaf and stem appliqués and Nine Patch blocks

1 rectangle, 4" x 8", *each* of 65 to 70 assorted red, orchid, peach, yellow, pink, blue, aqua, and orange prints for Nine Patch blocks

⅝ yard of yellow solid for binding

7⅞ yards of fabric for backing

84" x 97" piece of batting

2½ yards of 16"-wide fusible web (optional)

Thread or 6-strand embroidery floss in coordinating colors for appliqués and appliqué details

❖ CUTTING

All measurements include ¼"-wide seam allowances. Cut all strips across the width of fabric unless otherwise indicated.

From the cream solid, cut:

◆ 5 strips, 10" x 42"; crosscut into 20 squares, 10" x 10"

◆ 11 strips, 3½" x 42"; crosscut into 120 squares, 3½" x 3½"

◆ 5 squares, 14¼" x 14¼"; cut twice diagonally to yield 20 triangles. (You'll have 2 extra triangles.)

◆ 2 squares, 7½" x 7½"; cut once diagonally to yield 4 triangles

From the assorted green prints, cut a *total* of:

◆ 20 squares, 3½" x 3½"

From the assorted red, orchid, peach, yellow, pink, blue, aqua, and orange prints, cut a *total* of:

◆ 130 squares, 3½" x 3½"

From the aqua floral, cut:

◆ 8 strips, 2" x 42"

From the *lengthwise* grain of the yellow floral, cut:

◆ 4 strips, 6¼" x 85"

From the yellow solid, cut:

◆ 9 strips, 2" x 42"

APPLIQUÉING THE BLOCKS

1. Choose your favorite appliqué method and make appliqué templates for the tulip, leaves, and stem by tracing the pattern on page 84. Refer to "Appliqué Techniques" on page 7 for details as needed. Make the quantity indicated on the pattern for each shape. Refer to the photo on page 80 for color-placement ideas.

2. Using the pattern, make a placement guide and position the tulips, leaves, and stems on the 10" cream squares. Be sure the cream squares are positioned on point. Appliqué the shapes in numerical order as indicated on the pattern. Leave the bottom of leaf 3 unstitched; it will be sewn into the seam line. To add the stitching-line details, use a straight stitch or a small zigzag stitch on your machine, or hand embroider a stem stitch.

3. Make 20 appliqué blocks. Gently press and then trim each block to 9½" x 9½", referring to "Squaring Up Blocks" on page 7.

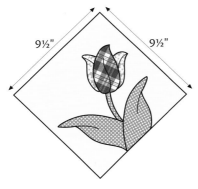

Make 20.

MAKING THE NINE PATCH BLOCKS

Using the 3½" cream squares and the additional 3½" squares of assorted colors, arrange the pieces in three rows as shown, randomly arranging the colored squares. Sew the squares in each row together, pressing the seam allowances toward the dark squares. Sew the rows together to make a Nine Patch block; press. Make 30 blocks.

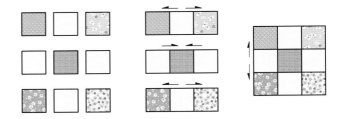

QUILT-TOP ASSEMBLY

For detailed instructions, refer to "Quilts Set Diagonally" on page 14. The setting triangles have been cut slightly oversize. You will trim them after the quilt center is assembled.

1. Refer to the quilt assembly diagram to arrange the Tulip blocks, the Nine Patch blocks, and the cream triangles cut from 14¼" squares in diagonal rows as shown.

2. Sew the pieces in each row together. Press the seam allowances toward the Tulip blocks. Sew the rows together and press the seam allowances in one direction. Add the cream triangles cut from 7½" squares to the corners last; press the seam allowances toward the corners.

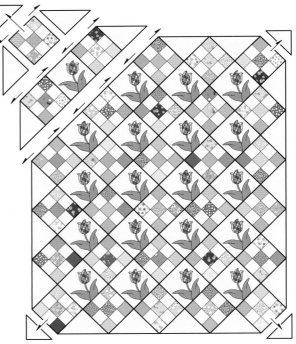

Quilt assembly

3. To trim and straighten the quilt top, align the ¼" mark on your ruler with the outermost points of the Nine Patch blocks. Use a rotary cutter to trim any excess fabric, leaving a ¼"-wide seam allowance. Square the corners of the quilt top as necessary.

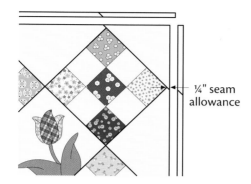

¼" seam allowance

4. Refer to "Borders" on page 15 to measure, cut, and sew the 2"-wide aqua floral strips for the inner border and then the 6¼"-wide yellow floral strips for the outer border. Press all seam allowances toward the newly added border strips.

⊞ FINISHING THE QUILT

Referring to "Finishing Techniques" on page 16, cut and piece the backing fabric and then layer the quilt top with batting and backing. After basting the layers together, hand or machine quilt as desired; see the quilting suggestion below. Trim the batting and backing so that the edges are even with the quilt top. Using the 2"-wide yellow strips, sew the binding to the quilt.

Quilting Suggestion

83

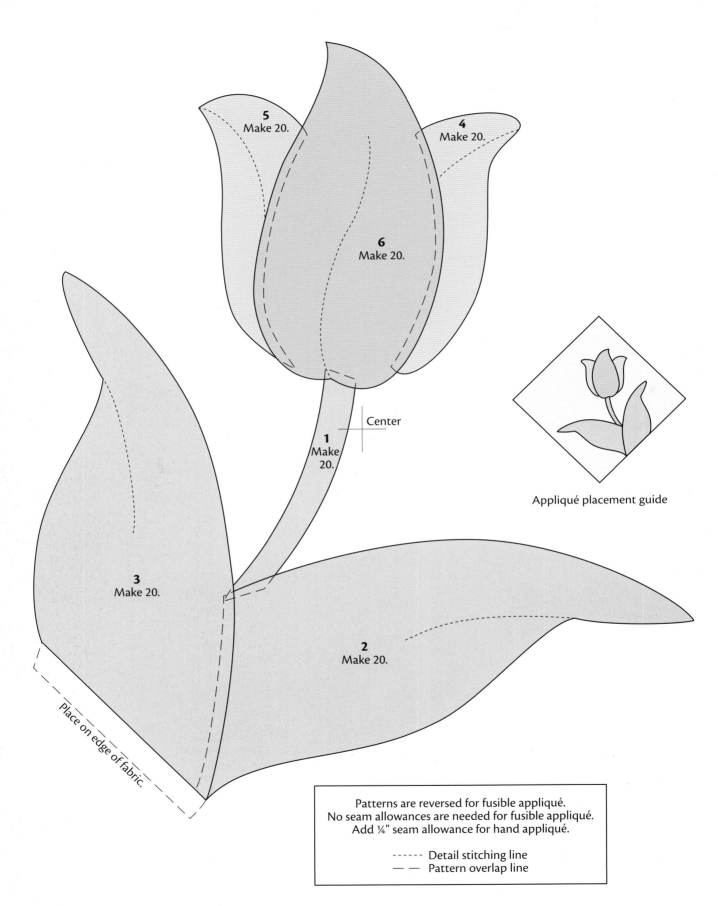

5 Make 20.

4 Make 20.

6 Make 20.

1 Make 20.

Center

Appliqué placement guide

3 Make 20.

Place on edge of fabric.

2 Make 20.

Patterns are reversed for fusible appliqué.
No seam allowances are needed for fusible appliqué.
Add ¼" seam allowance for hand appliqué.

----- Detail stitching line
— — Pattern overlap line

HOUSE ON THE HILL

Made by Nancy Mahoney.

Finished Quilt Size: 43½" x 43½" ◆ Finished Block Size: 9"

This enchanting appliqué pattern may or may not be an Alice Brooks design. The pattern has been attributed to her name and called Miniature Village. However, the 1930s Miniature Village pattern I found didn't have a byline. I also have this same appliqué pattern labeled House on the Hill, which is the name I chose for my quilt. Whatever you call it, it's a cute pattern and makes a cheery and appealing wall hanging. I selected different fabrics for all the houses and used a wide sashing, often seen in quilts from the '30s. A simple outer border was all that was needed to showcase these sweet little hilltop homes.

MATERIALS

Yardages are based on 42"-wide fabrics. Fat quarters measure 18" x 21" and fat eighths measure 9" x 21".

1⅛ yards of cream solid for block backgrounds, sashing squares, and corner squares

1 yard of purple print for outer border and binding

½ yard of green floral for sashing

1 fat quarter of brown print for roof appliqués

1 fat eighth of rust print for door and chimney appliqués

1 rectangle, 5" x 7", *each* of assorted prints—2 blue, 2 purple, 1 peach, 1 orange, 3 red and/or pink— for house appliqués

1 rectangle, 4" x 6", *each* of 9 assorted green prints for tree appliqués

3 yards of fabric for backing

49" x 49" piece of batting

1¼ yards of 16"-wide fusible web (optional)

2¾ yards of green baby rickrack (¼") for hill detail

Thread in coordinating colors for appliqués

Black thread or 6-strand embroidery floss for appliqué details

Black Pigma pen (size 05) for appliqué details

Fabric glue for attaching rickrack

CUTTING

All measurements include ¼"-wide seam allowances. Cut all strips across the width of fabric.

From the cream solid, cut:

◆ 3 strips, 10" x 42"; crosscut into 9 squares, 10" x 10"

◆ 1 strip, 2½" x 42"; crosscut into 16 squares, 2½" x 2½"

◆ 4 squares, 4½" x 4½"

From the green floral, cut:

◆ 6 strips, 2½" x 42"; crosscut into 24 pieces, 2½" x 9½"

From the purple print, cut:

◆ 4 strips, 4½" x 42"

◆ 5 binding strips, 2" x 42"

⬛ Appliquéing the Blocks

1. Choose your favorite appliqué method and make appliqué templates for the house, roof, door, chimney, and trees by tracing the pattern on page 89. Refer to "Appliqué Techniques" on page 7 for details as needed. Make the quantity indicated on the pattern for each shape. Refer to the photo on page 85 for color-placement ideas.

2. Using the pattern as a placement guide, position the houses, roofs, doors, chimneys, and trees on the 10" cream squares. Appliqué the shapes in numerical order as indicated on the pattern. To add the stitching-line details, use the Pigma pen to trace the details and then sew over the line with a straight stitch on your machine or hand embroider a stem stitch.

3. Cut the rickrack into nine pieces, 10½" long. Position a piece of rickrack as shown in the pattern and use a little fabric glue to hold it in place. Then stitch a straight stitch down the middle of the rickrack or use a zigzag stitch. (You'll need to adjust the width and length of the zigzag stitch so that as the needle swings left and right it crosses the rickrack as shown. Sew slowly, making minor adjustments as you stitch.)

4. Make nine appliqué blocks. Gently press and then trim each block to 9½" x 9½", referring to "Squaring Up Blocks" on page 7.

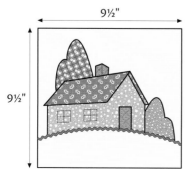

Make 9.

⬛ Quilt-Top Assembly

For detailed instructions, refer to "Quilts with Sashing Strips" on page 14.

1. Arrange and sew together four 2½" x 9½" green floral pieces and three blocks, alternating them as shown to make a block row; press. Make three rows.

Make 3.

2. Arrange and sew together three 2½" x 9½" green floral pieces and four 2½" cream squares as shown to make a sashing row; press. Make four rows.

Make 4.

3. Sew the block rows and sashing rows together, alternating them as shown in the quilt assembly diagram. Press the seam allowances toward the sashing rows.

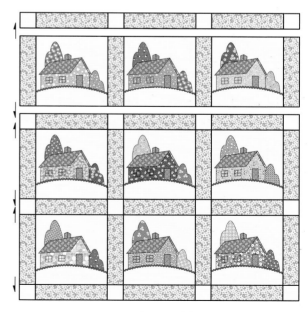

Quilt assembly

4. Measure the quilt through the center from side to side and from top to bottom. If the measurements differ, calculate the average and consider this the length. Trim the 4½" x 42" purple strips to that measurement. Sew an outer-border strip to the side edges of the quilt top. Sew a 4½" cream square to the ends of each remaining border strip, and then sew them to the top and bottom of the quilt top. Press all seam allowances toward the outer-border strips.

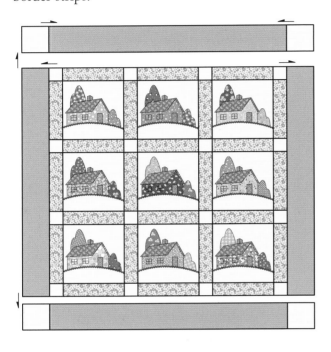

FINISHING THE QUILT

Referring to "Finishing Techniques" on page 16, cut and piece the backing fabric and then layer the quilt top with batting and backing. After basting the layers together, hand or machine quilt as desired; see the quilting suggestion below. Trim the batting and backing so that the edges are even with the quilt top. Using the 2"-wide purple strips, sew the binding to the quilt.

Quilting Suggestion

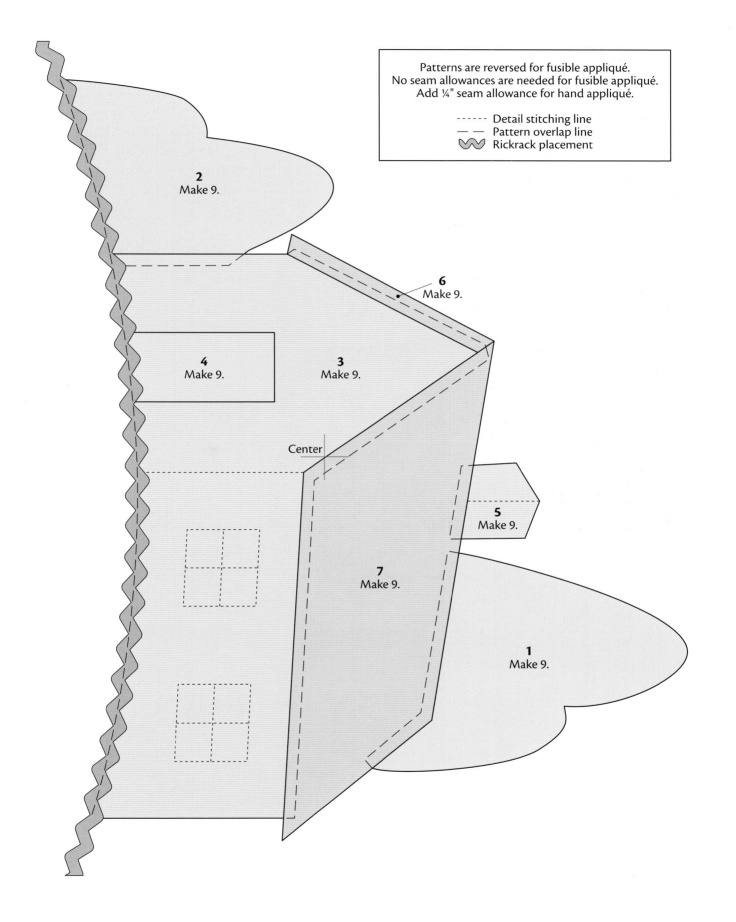

Patterns are reversed for fusible appliqué.
No seam allowances are needed for fusible appliqué.
Add ¼" seam allowance for hand appliqué.

- - - - - Detail stitching line
— — Pattern overlap line
〰 Rickrack placement

2
Make 9.

6
Make 9.

4
Make 9.

3
Make 9.

Center

5
Make 9.

7
Make 9.

1
Make 9.

COWBOY DAYS

Made by Nancy Mahoney.

Finished Quilt Size: 45" x 56" ◆ Finished Block Size: 9½"

The designer of this classic 1930s pattern is not known, but given the similarity to the Cowboy block on page 57, it's possible it was an Alice Brooks design. When I found these patterns, I couldn't believe my good fortune. As I child, I adored anything with horses! So I set out to design a quilt that every little buckaroo would love. I chose bright red scraps for the cowboys and one dark blue print for the horses; then I folded red fabric squares into triangles and tucked them in the corners to make three-dimensional Snowball blocks. Using the same dark blue print in the sashing and outer border, with a red border for accent, completes the design and makes this rousing quilt a winner.

MATERIALS

Yardages are based on 42"-wide fabrics.

1½ yards of dark blue leaf print for sashing, outer border, and binding

1⅓ yards of cream solid for block backgrounds

½ yard of red print 2 for inner border

⅜ yard of dark blue print for horse appliqués

⅓ yard of red print 1 for blocks

⅛ yard of light blue print for sashing squares

1 rectangle, 6" x 8", *each* of 6 red prints for cowboy appliqués

Scraps of black solid for cowboy boot appliqués

3⅛ yards of fabric for backing

50" x 61" piece of batting

1½ yards of 16"-wide fusible web (optional)

Thread in coordinating colors for appliqués

Black thread and/or 6-strand embroidery floss for appliqué details

Black Pigma pen (size 05) for appliqué details

CUTTING

All measurements include ¼"-wide seam allowances.
Cut all strips across the width of fabric unless otherwise indicated.

From the cream solid, cut:

- 4 strips, 10½" x 42"; crosscut into 12 squares, 10½" x 10½"

From red print 1, cut:

- 3 strips, 2½" x 42"; crosscut into 48 squares, 2½" x 2½"

From the *lengthwise* grain of the dark blue leaf print, cut:

- 4 strips, 3½" x 54"
- 5 binding strips, 2" x 44"
- 31 pieces, 2" x 10"

From the light blue print, cut:

- 20 squares, 2" x 2"

From red print 2, cut:

- 5 strips, 2½" x 42"

▩ APPLIQUÉING THE BLOCKS

1. Choose your favorite appliqué method and make appliqué templates for the cowboy, boots, and horse by tracing the pattern on pages 94 and 95. Refer to "Appliqué Techniques" on page 7 for details as needed. Make the quantity indicated on the pattern for each shape. Refer to the photo on page 90 for color-placement ideas.

2. Using the pattern as a placement guide, position a horse shape on six of the 10" cream squares and the cowboy and boot shapes on the remaining cream squares. Appliqué the shapes in numerical order as indicated on the pattern. Use the Pigma pen to trace the details of each horse's mane and each cowboy's spurs. To add the stitching-line details on the horses and the cowboys' ropes, trace the lines using the Pigma pen and then sew over the line with a straight stitch on your machine or hand embroider a stem stitch. Use the Pigma pen to draw the horses' eyes; then use a small straight stitch on your machine to outline the eyes, or hand embroider a stem stitch and/or a French knot in the eye centers.

3. Make six cowboy appliqué blocks and six horse appliqué blocks. Gently press and then trim each block to 10" x 10", referring to "Squaring Up Blocks" on page 7.

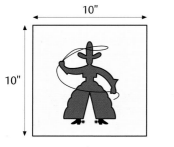

Make 6.

Make 6.

▩ COMPLETING THE BLOCKS

1. To make the folded corner triangles, fold the 2½" red squares in half diagonally, wrong sides together, and press, using steam. Make 48.

Fold.

2. With the raw edges aligned, place four folded triangles on the right side of each appliquéd block as shown. Pin and then baste, using a scant ¼"-wide seam allowance.

▩ QUILT-TOP ASSEMBLY

For detailed instructions, refer to "Quilts with Sashing Strips" on page 14.

1. Referring to the quilt assembly diagram, arrange and sew together four 2" x 10" dark blue pieces and three blocks, alternating them as shown to make a block row; press. Make a total of four rows—two with a horse in the middle and two with a cowboy in the middle.

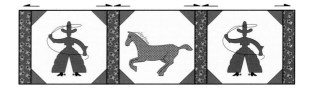

2. Arrange and sew together three 2" x 10" dark blue pieces and four 2" light blue squares as shown to make a sashing row; press. Make five rows.

Make 5.

3. Sew the block rows and sashing rows together, alternating them as shown. Press the seam allowances toward the sashing rows.

Quilt assembly

4. Refer to "Borders" on page 15 to measure, cut, and sew the 2½"-wide red strips for the inner border and then the 3½"-wide dark blue strips for the outer border. Press all seam allowances toward the newly added border strips.

FINISHING THE QUILT

Referring to "Finishing Techniques" on page 16, cut and piece the backing fabric and then layer the quilt top with batting and backing. After basting the layers together, hand or machine quilt as desired; see the quilting suggestion below. Trim the batting and backing so that the edges are even with the quilt top. Using the 2"-wide dark blue strips, sew the binding to the quilt.

Quilting Suggestion

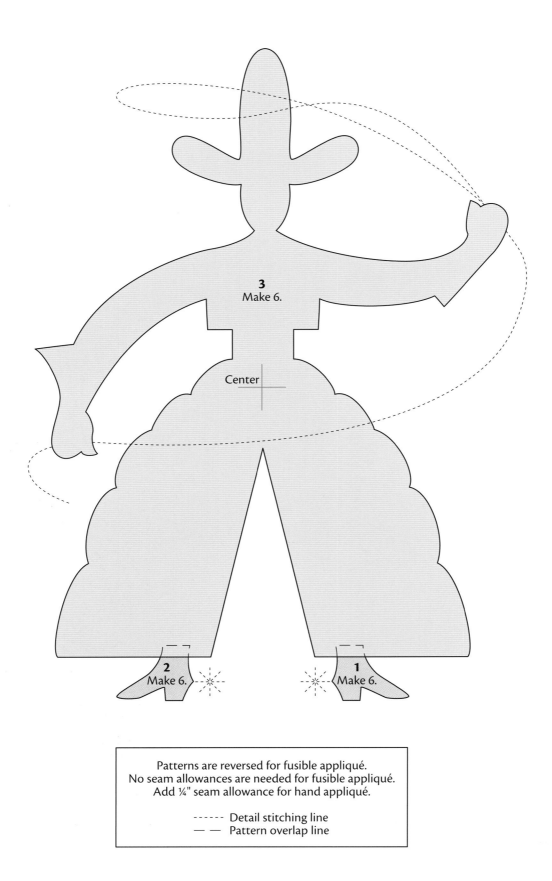

3
Make 6.

Center

2
Make 6.

1
Make 6.

Patterns are reversed for fusible appliqué.
No seam allowances are needed for fusible appliqué.
Add ¼" seam allowance for hand appliqué.

----- Detail stitching line
— — Pattern overlap line

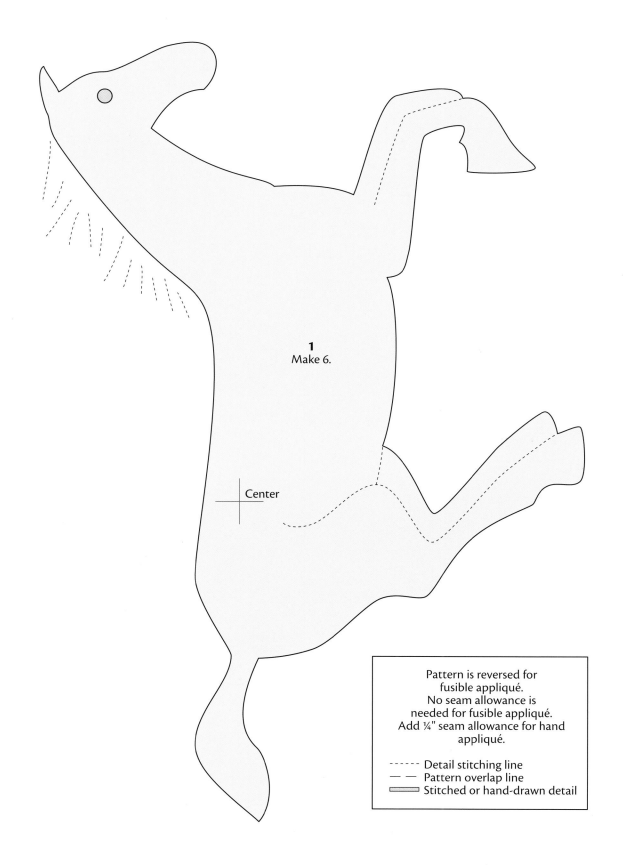

1
Make 6.

+ Center

Pattern is reversed for
fusible appliqué.
No seam allowance is
needed for fusible appliqué.
Add ¼" seam allowance for hand
appliqué.

----- Detail stitching line
— — Pattern overlap line
▬▬ Stitched or hand-drawn detail

ABOUT THE AUTHOR

Author, teacher, fabric designer, and award-winning quiltmaker, Nancy Mahoney has enjoyed making quilts for more than 20 years. An impressive range of her beautiful quilts has been featured in many national and international quilt magazines.

Appliqué Quilt Revival is Nancy's ninth book with Martingale & Company. Her other best-selling books include *Ribbon Star Quilts* (2008), *Square Deal* (2007), and *Quilt Revival* (2006).

Almost entirely self-taught, Nancy continues to explore new ways to combine traditional blocks and updated techniques to create quilts that are fun and easy to make.

Nancy lives in Florida with her life partner of over 30 years, Tom, and their umbrella cockatoo, Prince.

Please visit Nancy at www.nancymahoney.com.

Acknowledgments

A very special thanks to:

Tom Reichert, first and foremost, for encouraging me to continue what I love doing. What a guy!

The delightful people at Martingale & Company; they are always a joy to work with!

My special friends Julie Sheckman and Loretta Sylvester, who were incredibly kind to give up their free time to make quilts.

Dawn Kelly, Nannette Moore, Karen Housel, and Kelly Wise, who are all wonderful machine quilters. Their talent and imaginative quilting breathed life into these quilts. This book wouldn't have been possible without their help.

Kathy, Denise, Jan, Kelly, and everyone at The Sew and Quilt Shop in Bunnell, Florida—you're a great bunch of gals! I truly appreciate everyone's help, support, and encouragement.

The Memory Makers Quilt Guild—a fantastic group of women, whose enthusiastic oohs and aahs encourage me to try new things.

The following companies for generously providing so many great products: P&B Textiles and In The Beginning Fabrics, whose lovely fabrics created so many of the quilts; American & Efird and Marci Brier for Mettler and Signature threads; Hobbs Bonded Fibers and H. D. Wilbanks for their Heirloom cotton batting; the Warm Company for its outstanding fusible-web products; and Roxanne Products Company for its wonderful basting glue.